D1065519

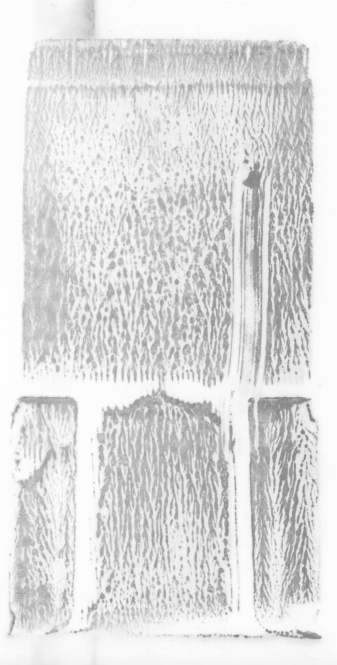

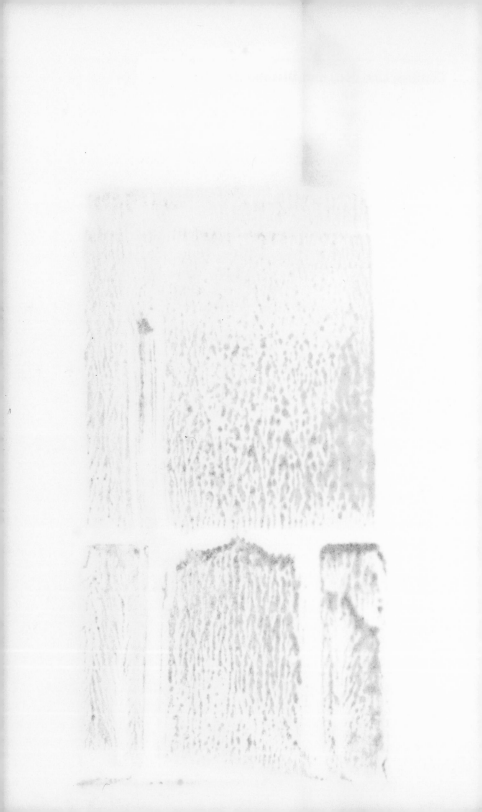

Conflict, Decision, and Dissonance

Stanford Studies in Psychology, III

Editors

Robert R. Sears
Leon Festinger
Douglas H. Lawrence

Conflict, Decision, and Dissonance

Leon Festinger

with the collaboration of

Vernon Allen
Marcia Braden
Lance Kirkpatrick Canon
Jon R. Davidson
Jon D. Jecker
Sara B. Kiesler
Elaine Walster

Stanford University Press, Stanford, California

Stanford University Press
Stanford, California
© 1964 by the Board of Trustees of the
Leland Stanford Junior University
Printed in the United States of America
Original edition 1964
Reprinted 1967

Foreword

It is often said that it is difficult to pursue a creative endeavor in isolation. If one is alone, one misses the exchange of ideas, the intellectual stimulation, the support and enthusiasm of active and interested colleagues. A group of persons working in the same general area, interacting and influencing one another, frequently provide an atmosphere in which ideas are easily produced and technical problems are readily solved. The research reported in this volume is the product of such a group.

This does not mean that we engaged in "group research." Indeed, we did not. Each experiment reported is the product of a person who had an idea, became enthusiastic about it, and was able to solve the problems of translating the idea into an experiment. The other people sometimes helped to stimulate the ideas, sometimes to support the enthusiasm, and frequently helped to clarify the problems. The research, however, was individual work. Those experiments which are co-authored are instances of true collaboration.

The group of persons involved in this research endeavor were mostly graduate students in the Psychology Department at Stanford University. The exception to this is Dr. Vernon Allen, whose experiment, reported in Chapter 3, was conducted during a year he spent at Stanford University on a Postdoctoral Research Fellowship from the National Institutes of Health of the United States Public Health Service. Dr. Allen is now on the faculty of the Department of Psychology of the University of Wisconsin.

Dr. Marcia Braden, at the time she worked on the experiment reported in Chapter 6, had just received her Ph.D., and worked on the experiment before leaving for the University of Pittsburgh where she is now a member of the faculty of the Department of Psychology.

Lance Kirkpatrick Canon is currently a graduate student. His experiment, reported in Chapter 4, was carried out while he held a Predoctoral Fellowship from the National Institutes of Health.

Jon R. Davidson is also, currently, a graduate student. His experiment, reported in Chapter 2, was done while he held a Fellowship for Graduate Study from the Woodrow Wilson Foundation. The experiment that is reported in Chapter 3 was carried out while he held a National Science Foundation Cooperative Graduate Fellowship.

Dr. Jon D. Jecker reports the results of two experiments in this volume, one in Chapter 2 and the other in Chapter 4. Both of these were done while he held a Predoctoral Fellowship from the National Institutes of Health. The experiment he reports in Chapter 4 is based on a thesis submitted in partial fulfillment of the requirements for the Ph.D. degree at Stanford University. Dr. Jecker is now in the Department of Psychology at Kent State University.

Sara B. Kiesler carried out the experiment reported in Chapter 2 while she held a fellowship from the Woodrow Wilson Foundation to do graduate work in Psychology. She is currently a graduate student in the Department of Psychology at Ohio State University. Lest this be misinterpreted by any reader, let me add that the move was made only to be with her husband, who moved there after receiving his Ph.D.

Dr. Elaine Walster reports four experiments in this volume. They are presented in Chapters 5 and 6. They were all carried out while she held a Predoctoral Fellowship from the National Institutes of Health. The second experiment in Chapter 5 is based on a thesis she submitted in partial fulfillment of the requirements for the Ph.D. degree at Stanford University. Dr. Walster is now a member of the Laboratory for Research in Social Relations at the University of Minnesota.

During the period of time in which this research was being done there were others who were working with us and who were important in maintaining an atmosphere of vitality for all of us. Although the research they did is not included in this volume because it does not fit the framework here, they nevertheless contributed to this volume while the research was in progress. These people are Dr. Jonathan Freedman, Dr. Charles Kiesler, Dr. Jane Allyn Hardyck, and Miss Judith R. Turner.

A number of other acknowledgments are also due. A number of people were indispensable in the planning and execution of the experiment reported by Walster in the second half of Chapter 5. These are Master Sergeant Shea at the Reception Center for the Sixth Army District located at Fort Ord, California, and Drs. Richard E. Snyder and John Caylor, both at the U.S. Army Leadership Human Research Unit, HUMRRO. The experiment by Jecker reported in Chapter 2 was helped considerably by the cooperation of Dr. A. B. Huntsman, superintendent of the Mountain View–Los Altos Union High School District, and Mr. John Wilkins, principal of the Los Altos High School. Appreciation is also due to Ian Dengler, William Blosser, Carl Langguth, and Michael Percival for their participation as confederates in the experiment reported by Jecker in Chapter 4.

Some of the experiments reported in this volume were not very expensive to carry out. Others were very expensive, indeed. We were very fortunate in having a grant from the Ford Foundation and another from the National Science Foundation (Grant No. G-11255) to support this work. I am very grateful to both these foundations for making it possible to do this research.

Lastly, I want to express thanks and appreciation to Dr. Harold B. Gerard, Dr. Edward E. Jones, and Dr. Douglas H. Lawrence. Each of these three persons read the manuscript carefully and thoughtfully. The suggestions and criticisms they offered helped materially to improve it.

LEON FESTINGER

Stanford University
October 1, 1963

Table of Contents

Conflict, Decision, and Dissonance

Chapter One

Introduction

■

How do human beings make decisions? This seemingly simple
question has been a major concern of psychologists for many
decades and of philosophers for centuries. In the eighteenth cen-
tury, for example, an argument raged as to whether or not the fact
that human beings could, and did, make choices implied a free will
which contradicted the idea of determinism. If a human being
could voluntarily decide which of several possible courses of action
he would pursue, then clearly he had free will and a deterministic
philosophy was untenable. The success of this argument, of course,
depended upon the assumption that the process of making a
choice, of making a decision, was inevitably surrounded with mys-
tery. Today, after much theorizing and experimentation and
study, much of the psychology of decision making is still not well
understood.

What is involved in "understanding" the psychology of decision
making? The traditional view in science is that one has an "understanding" of a process if one can predict the outcome accurately.
Can one, then, predict from *a priori* knowledge which of several
alternatives a person will choose when faced with a decision? In
some instances one can, but it turns out to be a trivial prediction.
If one obtains an accurate measurement of the net attractiveness
of each of the alternatives, one can predict with reasonable accu-
racy that the person will choose that alternative which is most
attractive.

In other instances, the prediction of choice is not such a simple
matter. The problem has been summarized very nicely by Restle
(1961) as follows:

The answer is very simple if the choice is merely between something the person likes and something he dislikes. Some doubt arises when the choice is more difficult, as when it is between two things which the individual likes and his preference is relatively slight. The question becomes difficult and interesting when the alternatives offered are complex, each involving some pleasant and some unpleasant aspects, or where the person chooses without being certain as to the outcome he will receive.

A large part of the relevant theory is found, not in psychology, but in mathematical economics, statistics and decision theory. These disciplines seek to give good advice to a rational decision-maker by telling him how to choose in complex or risky situations. The aim of the advice is to get the chooser to be as successful, on the average, as is possible, so that he will obtain all he can of whatever it is he wants. Such advice can be given only in conjunction with knowledge of the person's desires, which must be measured. A basic issue in decision theory is the measurement of desires or, as the term is used in that field, the measurement of utility. (Pp. 59–60.)

It is interesting to note that the real problem in the prediction of choice becomes a technical problem of measurement. If we do not have adequate measurement, or if the alternatives are complex so that we do not know how to combine their various aspects into a single measure of utility, then there is a problem for "decision theory." These problems may be interesting, but they are really not concerned with the question of how a person makes a decision. That entire question is taken care of with the assumption, undoubtedly valid, that the person will choose whichever alternative is more attractive to him.

Clearly, however, the prediction of which alternative will be chosen is a minor aspect of the psychological problem of decision making. The old paradox attributed to the fourteenth-century philosopher Buridan illustrates this very well. The paradox pictures a hungry animal who starves to death because it cannot reach a decision between two readily available, precisely equal piles of food. The problem is not which pile of food is chosen. The real problem concerns the process by which the organism evaluates the alternatives and *does* make a choice. There are many outcomes other than "which is chosen" that must be successfully predicted before one can "understand" the psychology of decision making. How will the person behave while in the pre-decision situation? What will his reaction be after the decision is made? What is the relation between pre-decision and post-decision behavior?

Even these three questions, broad as they are, do not adequately cover the entire psychological problem of decision making. Much work, for example, has been done on how long it takes to make a decision, what determines decision difficulty, confidence in decisions, the difference between decisions that involve positive or that involve negative alternatives, and the like. The three questions mentioned above, however, will serve as the focus of interest in this volume.

The pre-decision situation is generally regarded as one in which the person experiences conflict. The conflict exists, presumably, because of the simultaneous presence of at least two mutually incompatible response tendencies. Much of the theoretical thinking on the subject of decision situations has been concerned with how the person behaves during the period when he is in conflict, that is, before he has been able to come to a decision. Indeed, this pre-decision period can be, and has been, considered to be synonymous with a period of frustration. The kinds of behavior that have been pointed out and emphasized by writers such as Lewin (1935) and Miller (1944) are mainly reactions to the unpleasantness of such frustration. Anger and aggression, withdrawal from the situation, deterioration of performance, and an assortment of other behavior have been mentioned.

We shall not, however, spend time on these considerations. What concerns us primarily are the processes involved in reaching a decision, and not the reactions to frustration. Very few theoretical statements have been made about those aspects of behavior in the pre-decision situation that are instrumentally related to reaching a decision. The problem we are pointing to can be put very simply as a question: What is the person doing during the time it takes to make a decision that enables him to make the decision and determines what the decision is?

Although it is rarely stated explicitly, most people would probably agree that a good deal of behavior in the pre-decision period is devoted to the examination and evaluation of the various alternatives. That is, the person gathers information about the alternatives, evaluates and re-evaluates them, and compares their good and bad aspects. There are, however, no experimental data concerning this process and, if one gets down to the details, there is great unclarity. It is possible to maintain, for example, that the evaluation of the alternatives in the pre-decision period is a very systematic affair in the course of which the alternatives are re-interpreted so as to produce greater and greater divergence in attractiveness. When the divergence becomes great enough, the person is finally able to make a decision. The presumed partiality of the information gathering and evaluation is, thus, instrumental in allowing the person to reach a decision.

Another possible view, however, is that the information gathering and evaluation that occur in the pre-decision period are not biased at all, but are, on the contrary, highly objective and impartial. This view would hold that until the person makes his decision, implicitly or explicitly, he seeks to discover and evaluate objectively all the information that is reasonably available to him. When he has accumulated and evaluated enough information to make him sufficiently confident that the preference order he sees in the alternatives will not be reversed by additional information, he makes his decision. The closer together in attractiveness the alternatives are, and the more important the decision, the greater is the confidence he would like to have that additional information will not change the preference order. If this were an adequate description of the process, the pre-decision information gathering and evaluation would, indeed, be objective and impartial. There is some evidence from experiments by Irwin, Smith, and Mayfield (1956) and by Irwin and Smith (1956) to support this view, but the evidence is far from conclusive. It does, however, establish that the closer together the alternatives are in attractiveness, and the more variable is the information the person acquires about them, the more information the person seeks out before he is ready to make a decision.

On the whole, however, the problem simply exists as an important problem on which little has been said or done. We do not know whether or not behavior in the pre-decision period is instrumental in enabling the person to make a decision. We also do not know what the details of this decision process are and, if the process is instrumental, in what way it is.

Theoretical statements about what happens after a decision has been made and about the relationship between post-decision processes and pre-decision processes are equally rare. To the writer's knowledge, the earliest such statements were those of Kurt Lewin (1951). In discussing the reason for the effectiveness of group decisions in causing changes in behavior, Lewin states: ". . . a process like decision which takes only a few minutes is able to affect conduct for many months to come. The decision links motivation to action and, at the same time, seems to have a 'freezing' effect which is partly due to the individual's tendency to 'stick to his decision . . . .' " (P. 233.)

In other words, Lewin believed that simply making a decision exerted a stabilizing effect on the situation. The person then tended to behave in line with the decision, even if this were difficult to do.

In a slightly different context Lewin (1951) also said something about the relation between the pre- and the post-decision situations. In discussing the behavior of a housewife who buys food he states:

For example, if food is expensive, two forces of opposite direction act on the housewife. She is in a conflict. The force away from spending too much money keeps the food from going into that channel. A second force, corresponding to the attractiveness of the food tends to bring it into the channel.

Let us assume the housewife decides to buy an expensive piece of meat: the food passes the gate. Now the housewife will be very eager not to waste it. The forces formerly opposing one another will now both point in the same direction: the high price that tended to keep the expensive food out is now the reason why the housewife makes sure that through all the difficulties the meat gets safely to the table and is eaten. (P. 176.)

In other words, according to Lewin, the stronger the conflict before the decision, the greater the tendency to carry through on the decision afterward. The post-decision situation is dynamically different from, but intimately related to, the pre-decision situation.

Festinger's theory of cognitive dissonance (1957) carries this idea further in a more generalized way. According to this theory, the amount of dissonance that exists after a decision has been made is a direct function of the number of things the person knows that are inconsistent with that particular decision. It is clear from this, then, that the greater the conflict before the decision, the greater the dissonance afterward. Hence the more difficulty the person had in making the decision, the greater would be his tendency to justify that decision (reduce the dissonance) afterward. The decision can be justified by increasing the attractiveness of the chosen alternative and decreasing the attractiveness of the rejected alternative, and one would expect a post-decision cognitive process to occur that accomplishes this spreading apart of the attractiveness of the alternatives.

There are data that show that such a process does indeed take place. Experiments (Brehm, 1956; Brehm and Cohen, 1959; Brock, 1963) have shown quite conclusively that ratings of the attractiveness of the alternatives change so as to justify the decision. Ratings obtained after a decision has been made are spread apart as compared with ratings obtained before the decision was made. Furthermore, these studies have shown that the more difficult the decision, that is, the greater the pre-decision conflict, and hence the greater the post-decision dissonance, the larger is this dissonance-reduction effect.

These data, however, raise an important theoretical issue. In Festinger's theoretical position, one finds the implication that the cognitive process that results in the divergence of the attractiveness of the alternatives occurs only after the decision has been made, and not before. Other theoretical positions can exist which acknowledge the fact that the divergence in attractiveness of alternatives does occur, but maintain that the pre-decision and post-decision processes are *not* dynamically different. These theoretical positions would claim that the spreading apart begins during the pre-decision period in order to make the decision possible. The decision itself does nothing but involve the person in a commitment to a given course of action, and does not sharply alter the psychological processes that go on. After the decision there is still residual conflict, and the spreading-apart process continues, since conflict is unpleasant.

The point involved here is a very important one. If the same cognitive processes occur both before and after a decision, we can have a relatively simple theoretical framework capable of dealing with the entire process. In addition, such findings would imply that the "act of decision" is in no way critical from the point of view of the psychological process.

On the other hand, if post-decision processes are dynamically very different from pre-decision processes, if there is a sharp break in the kind of cognitive process that occurs, then a simple theoretical framework no longer suffices and we must recognize, and understand, the importance and psychological significance of the "act of decision." Up to now there have been no data that can be brought to bear squarely on this issue.

If one looks at the whole sequence of decision making, and at the theories and data that exist concerning it, one finds some knowledge, large areas of unclarity, and considerable theoretical disagreement. Our purpose in this book is to try to add some clarity to this area. We shall attempt to do this in two ways: by providing new experimental evidence concerning various stages of the decision-making process, and by explicating some ideas about the cognitive processes involved.

In the following chapters we shall report the results of ten original experiments that were conducted over a period of about three years. The orientation that guided this research was provided by the theory of cognitive dissonance. In general, we were concerned with taking a fresh look at the theory and some of its implications—where was the theory inadequate and in need of modification; where was it vague and in need of added precision; where were additional data needed?

The area in which we made headway was, of course, determined by the occurrence or absence of good ideas. It seemed important to us to be able to distinguish clearly between dissonance and conflict, assuming that such a distinction turned out to be tenable. We were fortunate in having some technical ideas, and some good luck, that enabled us to make progress in this direction.

It also seemed important to us to know more about the details of the process of dissonance reduction. Intuitively, it seemed that one did not always obtain smooth, uncomplicated, dissonance-reduction effects after a decision. Sometimes, indeed, one obtained the reverse, namely, a feeling of regret. How could this be understood within the context of the theory? Again, we were fortunate in having some insights that enabled us to make some progress.

As the experiments were done, new problems emerged and new ideas developed. Consequently, second experiments were done to clarify the results of the first experiments, and third ones helped to clarify the results of the second. The ten experiments do represent, broadly speaking, a coherent group of studies. They do not, however, constitute an exhaustive analysis of the decision process, nor do they bring forth a formal theoretical statement of the precise details of this process. We hope that they make some contribution toward casting new light on old problems.

Chapter Two

The Difference Between Conflict and Dissonance

■

In considering the questions we have raised about the process of decision making, one point is obviously more critical than any of the others: Is the post-decision cognitive process radically different from the pre-decision cognitive process or not? The answer to this question will go a long way in determining the structure of a coherent account of the nature of decision making. We shall, consequently, deal with this issue first.

Experiments concerned with testing implications from dissonance theory about the post-decision cognitive process have interpreted the divergence in attractiveness of the chosen and rejected alternatives after the decision as a good indication that the post-decision process is biased. The data, however, merely show that sometime between the pre-decision and post-decision measurements, a divergence in attractiveness has occurred. These data do not rule out the possibility that the divergence occurred before the decision was made. However, our own guess is that during the pre-decision period, when the person is in conflict, the information gathering and evaluative activities with respect to the alternatives are impartial and objective. By characterizing the pre-decision process as "impartial" and "objective" we do not mean that the person does not evaluate. We mean only that he does not *bias* his evaluations in favor of one alternative. Thus, although changes in the attractiveness of the alternatives may occur during this period, they would not be systematic. On the average, the difference in attractiveness between the alternatives would remain the same throughout the pre-decision period. One should not be able to observe any spreading apart of the attractiveness in favor of the to-be-chosen alternative. Once the decision is made, however, and dissonance-reduction processes begin, one should be able to observe that the difference in attractiveness between the alternatives changes, increasing in favor of the chosen alternative.

There exists, of course, a major technical problem of how one can test this implication of our hypothesis. The most direct means of experimental testing is, unfortunately, beset with difficulties. Let us examine the problem. Contemplate two experimental conditions. In each of them, subjects are given a choice between two alternatives whose attractiveness has been previously measured. In one of these conditions we would remeasure the attractiveness of the alternatives immediately before the person has made a decision, while in the other condition we would remeasure them immediately after the decision has been made. If we could accomplish this, we would have data adequate to evaluate our hypothesis.

How does one accomplish this experimentally, however? The difficulty arises, of course, in connection with the experimental condition in which remeasures are to be taken immediately before the decision. How can we identify this point objectively? At any point prior to an overt statement of the decision at which we interrupt for measurement, some people may already have made the decision implicitly, while others may be at such an early stage of the decision-making process that they are not even near the point of making a decision. The results of such an experiment would, consequently, be very ambiguous theoretically.

The best one could do along the lines of such a direct experimental test would be to arrange a situation somehow in which one could be reasonably sure that, at the point of interruption for measurement, no one had yet actually made a decision. One would then have a bit of a problem with the post-decision measurement condition, since one would want to ensure that, at approximately this same point in time, all of the persons in this condition would have actually made their decision. One cannot, with present experimental technology, completely achieve this and, consequently, one cannot eliminate all ambiguities from the results of such an experiment. One can, however, produce a situation that comes close to these requirements. Such an experiment is reported now by Davidson and Kiesler. Let us look at the means by which these technical problems were dealt with, and at the results. We will then consider further the extent to which the data support the theoretical implications in question.

Experiment

Cognitive Behavior Before and After Decisions

Jon R. Davidson and Sara B. Kiesler

According to Festinger's (1957) theory of cognitive dissonance, a re-evaluation of attitudes occurs after a decision in order to make relevant cognitions consistent with choice behavior. Festinger (1957), in making a sharp distinction between dissonance and conflict, implies that this process occurs only after the decision has been made and not before. Janis (1959), on the other hand, thinking in terms of "conflict resolution," implies that there is little or no distinction between pre- and post-decision behavior and that systematic re-evaluation occurs both before and after the decision.

To our knowledge, there has been only one attempt to do an experiment to test this theoretical issue. Brehm, Cohen, and Sears (1960) conducted an experiment in which the attractiveness of the alternatives involved in a decision was rated at three different times by each subject. The first rating occurred before the subjects knew that there was to be any choice; the second, just before they were asked to make their decision; and the final one, after the decision had been stated. The authors reasoned that if systematic re-evaluation of the alternatives occurred before the decision was made, it would be reflected in the second ratings—they would be significantly different from the first in the direction of favoring the to-be-chosen alternative. On the other hand, if such systematic re-evaluation occurred only after the decision, the second rating would be only randomly different from the first, and both of these would differ from the final rating.

The results of the study were equivocal. The final rating differed significantly from the first rating in the direction anticipated. The second rating, however, was between these other two, but was not significantly different from either. Taken at face value, this result would tend to support the idea that systematic re-evaluation of the alternatives occurs both before and after a decision has been made. The equivocation and ambiguity of interpretation lie in the weakness of the results and in two major methodological issues. First, it is not clear what the effect would be on the third rating of having already made *two* prior ratings. This might make it difficult for the subject to change his evaluation any more and might, thus, have lessened the change from the second to the third rating. Second, and more important, there was little control over the making of implicit decisions before, and perhaps during, the second rating. As a matter of fact, the procedure employed in the ratings would be likely to have encouraged the making of a decision. The procedure was a combination of rating and ranking. The subjects were instructed to indicate on a scale how attractive each alternative was but not to place any two of them at the same scale point. It is difficult to imagine that, if subjects knew which two alternatives they had to choose between, and were almost at the point of making a decision, the activity of ranking would not precipitate decisions at that time. Hence the results of this experiment cannot be accepted with much assurance on this issue.

It is clear that in order to obtain adequate data on this question, we must have an experimental procedure that works against the occurrence of any implicit decisions before the pre-decision measurement. Moreover, the pre-decision measurement itself must not be in a form that would encourage decisions at that time. On the other hand, the procedure must be one that produces conditions favorable for pre-decision re-evaluation of the alternatives, so that, if such a process does occur, it would show itself. It is somewhat unclear, theoretically, exactly what these favorable conditions would be. However, one thing does seem clear. If systematic pre-decision re-evaluation does occur, it would probably be facilitated by adequate time for reflection and consideration of the alternatives. An ordinary decision procedure might put pressure on the subject to decide too rapidly.

To meet these requirements, we used a decision situation in which items of information relevant to the decision were given to subjects sequentially. In order to avoid implicit decisions, all subjects were told that later they would receive really important information. Half the subjects were given the items of information in rapid sequence, so that they had relatively little time to reflect on them. The other half were given the items of information very slowly, so that there was considerable time for reflection and re-evaluation. Re-evaluation was measured for half the subjects before the decision and for the other half, after the decision. How well these objectives were achieved may be judged from the following detailed account of the procedure.

Procedure

The subjects for this experiment were 100 girls, ranging in age from 13 to 16, who were recruited from various youth organizations in the Palo Alto, California, area. The girls volunteered for the study and were not paid for their participation.

The experiment was conducted with groups of from two to six of these girls. When we started the study, an attempt was made to conduct the experiment on the premises of the youth organization to which each group belonged during a regular meeting time. Three groups were run in this manner, but the noise and distraction proved difficult to cope with under these conditions. The data from the 15 girls involved in these three groups were discarded. The remaining 85 girls were brought to the laboratory at Stanford University for the experiment.

When the subjects arrived at the laboratory they were seated at individual tables upon which the experimental materials were placed. After we had explained that we were interested in decision making, they were each asked to answer the questions in a six-page booklet. Each page briefly described a different decision-making situation and asked the subject to rank, in order of their importance for that decision, a list of "crucial factors."

The third page in this booklet contained the important question for the study. This page asked the subject to imagine herself "responsible for hiring a man to become a first vice president" in a firm she "owned and controlled." The subject was asked to rank eight qualities (e.g., leadership, experience, education, sociability) in order of their importance for this decision. The other questions on the other pages in the booklet were included simply to minimize the possibility of the subject's remembering exactly how she had ranked the qualities on the critical question.

After completing the booklet, the subjects were told that they would now consider, in greater detail, the specific decision of hiring a vice president. Two fictitious men, Mr. Brown and Mr. Jones, were applicants for the job. The subjects were told that they would be given information about these men on printed cards, and that they would receive, in sequence, a total of ten such cards to read. It was further stressed that the cards were arranged in order of increasing importance of the information on them. In particular, the last two cards they received would contain very important information. Hence, they were told, it would be "impossible" to reach any sort of "decent" decision until they had read all the cards. This was an attempt to minimize the extent to which subjects would make decisions early in the process of acquiring information. The instructions also stressed that the decisions were important and that they would be compared to the results obtained from other girls and from adults.

Information cards were then given to the subjects one at a time. Each card contained a statement saying that Mr. Jones excelled in one quality in which Mr. Brown was average, while Mr. Brown excelled in another quality in which Mr. Jones was average. There were, thus, two qualities mentioned on each of the four cards, covering the eight qualities that the subjects had previously ranked in terms of importance for the decision. Subjects actually received only four cards to read before re-measurements were taken and before they were asked to make their decisions. Thus, they knew that four of these previously ranked qualities were favorable to Mr. Jones and four of them favorable to Mr. Brown.

During the period of receiving and reading these four cards, one of the experimental manipulations was introduced. All subjects were allowed 45 seconds to read each card, but the amount of time between cards was varied. In the "short-deliberation-time" condition the subjects were given five seconds to think about the information before being handed the next card to read. In the "long-deliberation-time" condition they were allowed one minute after the first card, and two and one-half minutes after each of the next three cards, to think about the information.

At the end of the *deliberation time* for the fourth card the procedure was interrupted, the experimenter explaining that he was interested in seeing what they were thinking "at this stage of the game." At this point, the second experimental variable was manipulated.

Post-Decision Measurement Condition. Subjects in this condition were told that although we had cautioned them not to make any decisions before reading all the material, we wanted to know what they were thinking now. They were asked to write down which of the two, Mr. Jones or Mr. Brown, they would hire at this point. These decision statements were collected and, after a two-minute wait during which the experimenter busied himself with various things, they were asked to answer an exact duplicate of page three of the pre-questionnaire booklet. Thus, for this group the eight qualities were reranked after a decision.

Pre-Decision Measurement Condition. Subjects in this condition were given *exactly the same instructions* as those in the previous condition, except that the order of events was inverted. They were first asked to rank the eight qualities and, after this task had been completed, were asked to make their decision. Thus, for this condition the eight qualities were reranked before the decision and, presumably, before any implicit decisions had been made by the subjects. All subjects, it should be remembered, were expecting to continue to read six more cards, the last two of which would contain particularly important information.

The subjects were then told that the experiment was actually finished. Before receiving any explanation, they were asked to answer a few questions primarily intended to determine the effectiveness of the experimental procedure and manipulations. The procedures and purposes of the experiment were then fully explained to the subjects.

The design of the experiment may be summarized by listing the four experimental conditions produced by our two manipulated variables. These are

> Short Deliberation Time–Pre-Decision Measurement,
> Short Deliberation Time–Post-Decision Measurement,
> Long Deliberation Time–Pre-Decision Measurement,
> Long Deliberation Time–Post-Decision Measurement.

A total of 84 subjects was run, 21 in each of these four experimental conditions. Of the 85 subjects available, one had to be discarded because of complete failure to comprehend the instructions and failure even to answer the pre-questionnaire. None of the 84 subjects who provided the data used in the analysis revealed any signs of suspicion or any sign of not having accepted the procedure at face value.

Results

We are primarily interested in comparing the four experimental conditions on the extent to which there is systematic re-evaluation of the alternatives involved in the decision. The relevant data can, of course, be obtained from a comparison of the pre-questionnaire ranking of the eight qualities with the reranking of these same eight qualities. It will be recalled that the subjects received information telling them that Mr. Jones excelled in four of these qualities while Mr. Brown excelled in the other four. The initial "attractiveness" of the two candidates for the job can, hence, be measured in terms of the sum of the ranks given to those qualities favoring each of them. The final "attractiveness" of the two candidates can be similarly computed from the reranking. Thus, for example, a subject may have initially ranked the eight qualities so that the four which turned out to favor Mr. Jones appeared in rank positions 2, 3, 5, and 6 in order of their importance for the job. Thus, the attractiveness of Mr. Jones would be 16 and the attractiveness of Mr. Brown would necessarily be 20, the sum of the remaining ranks 1, 4, 7, and 8.

Let us imagine that this subject, on the reranking, ranked the qualities favoring Mr. Jones as 1, 3, 4, and 5. The final attractiveness of Mr. Jones would thus be 13, a change of three units. If this subject actually decided in favor of Mr. Jones, this would be a change in a positive direction, that is, in the direction of increasing the difference in attractiveness to favor the alternative chosen or to be chosen. If the subject actually decided in favor of Mr. Brown, it would be scored as a change in a negative direction.

The direction of change, positive or negative, is obviously clear and unequivocal. The measure of the magnitude of this change, however, requires additional consideration. There was wide variation, of course, in how different subjects initially ranked the eight qualities. Different subjects could, hence, have changed by very different amounts. It seems reasonable, therefore, to construct an index by dividing the change in the sum of ranks of the qualities favoring the chosen person by the maximum possible change in that direction, thus obtaining a value for each person that could lie only between −1 and +1. Thus, in our example, the maximum change in the direction of favoring Mr. Jones would be a change from the initial score of 16 to a best possible final score of 10 (the sum of the ranks of 1, 2, 3, and 4). Since this subject chose Mr. Jones, his index value would be his actual change of +3 divided by this maximum possible change of 6, or +.50.

Imagine a different subject who had the same initial ranking and the same final ranking of the eight qualities, but who chose

TABLE 2.1

Average Indices of Re-evaluation of Alternatives

| | Measurement | |
Deliberation Time	Pre-Decision	Post-Decision
Short	+.03	+.21
Long	+.09	+.41

Mr. Brown. This subject would have changed three units in a negative direction out of a possible ten units (initial sum of ranks of 20 for the four qualities favoring Brown to a final possible sum equaling 10) and would be given an index value of −.30 to represent his change.

Table 2.1 presents the average of these index values for each of the experimental conditions. It seems, in the data, that both experimental variables have had an effect, but the more striking effect is determined by whether the re-evaluation of the alternatives is measured before or after the actual decision. An analysis of variance yields an F of 14.92 for this variable which, for 1 and 80 degrees of freedom, is significant well beyond the 1 per cent level. It is clear that before the decision is actually made, there is little systematic re-evaluation of the alternatives, +.03 in the short-deliberation-time condition and +.09 in the long-deliberation-time condition. After the decision the corresponding figures are +.21 and +.41. Certainly pre-decision processes, at least up to the point at which they were measured in this experiment, contribute very little, if at all, to the total systematic re-evaluation of alternatives that one observes after the decision.

It must be pointed out, however, that on the basis of these data one cannot say unequivocally that pre-decision processes contribute nothing to systematic re-evaluation of the alternatives. In the long-deliberation-time condition the pre-decision measurement of +.09 is significantly different from no change at about the 2 per cent level. Certainly, a change of this magnitude seems very small in comparison with the corresponding post-decision measurement of +.41, but it is nevertheless there. In the short-deliberation-time condition it is clear that there is no pre-decision systematic re-evaluation whatsoever. The significant change in the long-deliberation-time condition may be due to a tendency, when there is a lot of time to think, to make tentative decisions in spite of the instructions to the contrary. Or, as far as we can tell from these data, it may reflect a true pre-decision process. At any rate, its effect is minor.

Let us now turn our attention to the effect of the deliberation-time variable. Analysis of variance shows that its effect is significant at the 6 per cent level. This difference, however, is almost entirely due to the post-decision conditions. The short- and long-deliberation-time conditions do not differ significantly on the pre-decision measurements ($t = 0.92$). The difference on the post-decision measurements, however, yields a t of 1.95, which is significant at the 6 per cent level. This is an interesting and unanticipated effect. Although the difference in how much time they deliberated has only a negligible effect on what happens before the decision, it has a relatively large impact on what happens after the decision. It should be stressed that the period between the decision and the post-decision measurement was always the same, namely, two minutes. Consequently, the data suggest the possibility that the more thoroughly the alternatives have been considered and thought through prior to the decision, the more rapidly, or more effectively, can dissonance reduction proceed after the decision. On the basis of these data, however, this cannot be regarded as anything more than a suggestion.

It is worthwhile to point out that the results presented in Table 2.1 do not depend upon the particular index we chose as the measure of systematic re-evaluation of alternatives. The same statistical analyses were performed using simply the absolute change in the sum of ranks of the chosen or to-be-chosen alternative, and almost identical results were obtained.

It will be recalled from the procedure that after the subjects had been told that the experiment was actually completed, but before its purposes were explained to them, they were asked a few questions intended to assess the effectiveness of the experimental manipulations. In answer to one of these they were to write down all the qualities they could remember that were favorable to Mr. Jones and all that were favorable to Mr. Brown. It was expected that if the difference in deliberation time were really effective in the way intended, then subjects in the long-deliberation-time conditions should have better over-all memory than those in the short-deliberation-time conditions. After all, the former had considerably more time to think about and review the information they obtained. This turns out, of course, to be the case. The subjects in the two short-deliberation-time conditions remember and correctly associate with the job candidate an average of 5.3 out of a possible eight qualities. The subjects in the long-deliberation-time conditions remember an average of 6.4 of the eight qualities correctly, a difference that is statistically significant well beyond the 1 per cent level. From the point of view of this measure, no distinction can be made between the pre- and the post-decision measurement conditions. The measure of recall was obtained after they had all made their decisions.

One may also look at another aspect of the recall data. The extent to which the subjects remember consonant items (the four qualities favorable to the chosen candidate) as compared with dissonant items (the four qualities favorable to the rejected candidate) should also reflect post-decision dissonance reduction. Since the recall measure was obtained after subjects in all conditions had made their decisions, we would not expect any differences here between the pre- and the post-decision conditions unless the simple inversion in order between decision and rerating had some unanticipated effect. The data show that there are, indeed, no differences between the pre- and post-decision conditions at this point. The recall data do, however, show a uniform dissonance-reduction effect. More consonant than dissonant items were remembered by the subjects. In both the pre- and the post-decision conditions they remember an average of 3.1 consonant items and an average of 2.8 dissonant ones.

Summary

Eighty-four subjects were asked to choose which of two persons they would hire for a given position. Half the subjects were given little time to consider information before being asked to make the decision; the other half were given considerable time. Within each of these conditions, a measurement of the change in evaluation of the two job candidates was obtained before the decision for half the subjects and after the decision for the other half.

The results show that before the decision there is little or no systematic re-evaluation to favor the to-be-chosen alternative. After the decision, systematic re-evaluation does occur.

The data lend support to the theoretical position that pre-decision and post-decision processes are dynamically different.

Do the data from the Davidson and Kiesler experiment settle the question concerning the difference in cognitive re-evaluation processes before and after decisions? Certainly they lend support to the idea that a systematic spreading apart of the alternatives does *not* occur during conflict, but that this process does occur after a decision as a reaction to the existence of dissonance. But, unfortunately, these data certainly do not settle the issue. Let us examine the possible arguments of one who wanted to maintain a "conflict-resolution" hypothesis in the face of these results.

Two major points can be made that would enable one to maintain such a position plausibly. First, it can be pointed out that in the long-deliberation-time condition, where circumstances were presumably more favorable to pre-decision re-evaluation, there was, indeed, a significant change. Although this change was very small in magnitude, nevertheless it was there. And the very fact that it was very small in magnitude compared to the changes measured after the decision brings us to the second point. In the Davidson and Kiesler experiment, the subjects were expecting to receive more information of increasing importance and had been told not to make a decision until they had seen all the information. In other words, they were suspending judgment. In what sense, then, could one say that they were in a conflict situation? It seems quite plausible to argue that they were simply acting as information processors and did not enter a conflict–decision situation until they were asked to make their decision. It is, hence, not surprising that one does not see evidence of much conflict resolution before the person has fully entered the conflict situation. It is perfectly consistent with the data to maintain that a goodly portion of the re-evaluation change that was observed in the post-decision measurement could have occurred between the time they were told to make their decision and the time they actually made it.

Interpretation of the data is, hence, equivocal. But equivocation is inherent in this kind of design for testing this theoretical issue. If the experimenters had not used techniques that discouraged subjects from making early implicit decisions, any change that might be observed on a measurement before the overt decision was made would be open to question. With such techniques, which were probably successful by and large, there is no way of knowing whether the period between being asked to make the decision and making the decision is, or is not, particularly critical from the point of view of re-evaluation of the alternatives in a systematic manner.

If one is to settle the question of the difference or similarity between conflict-resolution processes and dissonance-reduction processes, one must obviously look for some quite different experimental vehicle. Actual comparisons of before and after measurements simply will not do the job. The Davidson and Kiesler experiment comes as close to answering the question as such a design probably will permit. But what is the more adequate experimental design that can give us less equivocal data?

It must be emphasized that the equivocation in the interpretation of such data centers around the uncertainty about precisely when the person is in a conflict situation and precisely when the decision is made. Hence it seems clear that a more adequate design must content itself with relying solely on post-decision measurement of re-evaluation of the alternatives. After the overt decision has been stated, one is at least certain that the person has gone through a conflict situation and has made the decision.

The following type of design for an experiment suggests itself. One would want to create an experimental situation where the degree to which the pre-decision and post-decision processes operate could be manipulated orthogonally. If this could be done, one could create one condition in which pre-decision processes would operate maximally and one where they would operate minimally. Cutting across these two conditions would be two others, one in which post-decision processes operated maximally and one in which they operated minimally. Thus, for example, the following four experimental conditions, if they could be achieved, ought to provide a good answer to our theoretical question:

1. Strong pre-decision conflict followed by high post-decision dissonance.

2. Strong pre-decision conflict followed by low post-decision dissonance.

3. Weak pre-decision conflict followed by high post-decision dissonance.

4. Weak pre-decision conflict followed by low post-decision dissonance.

Such an experiment is reported below by Jecker.

Experiment

The Cognitive Effects of Conflict and Dissonance

Jon D. Jecker

Many conflict theories would hold that if one must choose between two nearly equally desirable alternatives, the business of conflict resolution is to re-evaluate the alternatives so as to provide a clear basis for the choice. In order to be able to make the choice, the person makes the to-be-chosen alternative more desirable or the to-be-rejected alternative less desirable, or both. Moreover, one would expect that the greater the conflict the person experiences, the greater would be the tendency to create a clear difference between the alternatives before choosing.

A theory of conflict that was elaborated along such lines would, then, emerge with essentially the same predictions as dissonance theory about the end result of a process of re-evaluation of alternatives. What is more, both theories imply that the magnitude of the re-evaluation effect is responsive to the same variables, by and large. The more nearly equal in attractiveness the alternatives are, the greater is the degree of conflict and also the greater is the magnitude of dissonance after the decision. Hence, both theories would predict that the more nearly equal in attractiveness the alternatives were to start, the greater would be the amount of spreading apart of the alternatives, either to resolve the conflict or to reduce the post-decision dissonance. Similarly, both theories would expect the same effect from increasing the importance of the decision, which also increases both pre-decision conflict and post-decision dissonance.

How, then, can we choose between these two theories without attempting the impossible task of pinpointing in time, for each person, exactly when a decision is reached and interpolating measurement at precisely the proper time? Clearly, one must vary the degree of conflict in a manner that does not, at the same time, affect the magnitude of dissonance. One must also devise some way of varying the magnitude of post-decision dissonance that does not depend upon the prior existence of different degrees of pre-decision conflict. If this can be done, then clearly the two theoretical positions make very different predictions.

Most people would agree that a choice between two relatively attractive alternatives produces a conflict situation only if the alternatives are mutually exclusive, that is, if the person can have only one and not both. If the person is to receive both alternatives, the act of stating a choice is trivial and no conflict is involved. This, of course, suggests a means for manipulating the degree of conflict experienced without affecting the post-decision dissonance. One group of subjects, when making the choice, could be under the impression that they were virtually certain to get both alternatives. Another group could be under the impression that it was virtually certain that they would get only one alternative, namely, the one they chose. The latter group should experience more conflict during the decision-making process. If subjects actually receive only the alternative they chose, dissonance should be present in the same amount for both groups. Similarly, if subjects actually receive *both* alternatives following their decision, dissonance should be absent for both groups.

A theory of conflict resolution would lead one to expect to observe a systematic re-evaluation of the alternatives mainly in the high-conflict conditions irrespective of whether the subject actually received one or both alternatives. Dissonance theory would lead us to expect to observe systematic re-evaluation of the alternatives in the conditions in which the subjects received only the chosen alternative, irrespective of the degree of conflict involved in the decision.

Procedure

One hundred eight female high school students were the subjects in the experiment. The first twenty of these were used for preliminary testing for the purpose of modifying the instructions and the wording of questions to make them appropriate for these particular subjects. Eighty-eight subjects were run in the final experiment with the standardized procedure.

Each girl came individually to the room used for the experiment. The experimenter introduced himself as a graduate student in the Department of Psychology at Stanford University and explained that he was doing some market research in order to collect information about how people were reacting to the popular phonograph records currently on the market. He also told the subject that he was giving away gift records to the girls in exchange for their time spent helping in the reseach.

The subject was then shown fifteen records and asked to indicate whether or not she was familiar with each one, and which of them, if any, she already owned. After this, the subject was asked to rate each record on a seven-point scale according to how much she would like to have it. On the scale, zero was labeled "don't care," and 6 was described as "would rather have this record than any other record I can think of right now."

When the ratings had been completed the subjects were given instructions designed to vary the degree of conflict they would experience in making their choices. The experimenter told each subject that although he had planned to give each girl just one record as a gift, he now found that he had a few (or a lot of) extra records. Rather than return them to the record companies he would give a few (or a lot of) girls two records instead of one. The girls who were randomly assigned to the "high-conflict condition" were, of course, the ones who were told that there were few extra records. They were further told that one out of every twenty girls would be given two records. Those subjects who were assigned to the "low-conflict condition" were the ones who were told that there were many extra records. They were also told that 19 out of every 20 girls would receive two records. Whether she got only one record or two, each subject was told, would be determined by chance. She would draw a slip of paper out of a box on the table to decide. Depending upon the condition, the subjects were told either that the box contained 19 slips marked "1" and one slip marked "2," or that it contained 19 slips marked "2" and one marked "1."

Before the subject drew the slip of paper from the box, the experimenter showed her two records, told her that they would be the two she received if she were to get two records, and asked her to indicate which of the two she wanted in case she were to receive only one of them. The two records used as the choice alternatives were picked, for each subject, on the basis of her previous rating of them. The choice was always either between a record she had rated 3 and one she had rated 4 or between two that she had rated 4 and 5 on the scale of how much she wanted to have the record. Thus, each subject had a choice between records rated one unit apart in the "moderate" portion of the scale. Of course, any record she already owned was never used for the choice.

As the experimenter placed the two records in front of the subject for her to make her choice, he started a stop watch in his pocket. The watch was stopped when the subject clearly indicated her decision. Thus, a rather crude measure of decision time was obtained in order to have a check on the success of the high- versus the low-conflict manipulation. It was felt that it was better to content oneself with a rough measure than to make the timing procedure obvious and perhaps cause the girls to feel that they were supposed to make a quick decision.

After the decision had been made, the girl drew a slip of paper from the box on the table to find out whether she would get just the record she chose or both of them. The box from which she drew the slip of paper was "fixed" according to whether the subject was randomly assigned to the "no-dissonance" condition and was to obtain both records, or was assigned to the "dissonance" condition and was to get only the record she chose. Half of the subjects in each of the conflict conditions were assigned to each of the dissonance conditions.

After the slip of paper had been drawn, the experimenter gave the subject the record, or records, and asked her to wait a bit while he made some notes. After about two minutes, the experimenter told the girl that he was interested in a person's second thought about the phonograph records. He asked her to rate each of the 15 records again. The experimenter pointed out that after thinking about them, her ratings might or might not have changed. This did not matter. She was to rate them as she felt about them at this point.

This second rating concluded the experimental session. The subjects kept the records they had been given as gifts and they were asked not to talk about the experiment with others.

Of the 88 subjects who were run in the experiment, four had to be discarded from the data because, on the basis of their first ratings, there was no pair of records that met the criteria for choice alternatives. The data from another four subjects were discarded because these subjects chose the record that they had initially rated as less attractive. Whether this type of "inversion of choice" exists because of very unreliable use of the rating scale initially or because new considerations arise when they are faced with the choice is not clear. However, it is difficult to interpret the data from such subjects. This methodological issue has been extensively discussed by Brehm and Cohen (1962, pp. 123–26), and hence we shall not deal extensively with it here. The remaining 80 subjects were distributed evenly among the four experimental conditions, 20 subjects in each.

Results

Before discussing the results of the experiment it is important to know whether or not the manipulation of degree of conflict was successful. Although the idea of varying the degree of conflict by manipulating the extent to which the alternatives are mutually exclusive seems a plausible one, it is necessary to verify that it accomplished the intended result. To our knowledge, there is nothing in the experimental literature that would support the idea.

It has been generally accepted in the literature, and demonstrated in a variety of contexts, that the length of time it takes to make a decision does reflect the severity of conflict (Barker, 1942; Berlyne, 1960). We therefore obtained a rough measure of decision time as described in the procedure. If the manipulation did, indeed, affect the degree of conflict, then we would expect that in the high-conflict condition (low probability of obtaining both records) the decision time would be longer than in the low-conflict condition (high probability of obtaining both records). This proves to be the case. The measured decision time shows an average of 9.4 seconds in the high-conflict condition as compared with only 6.7 seconds in the low-conflict condition. The difference is significant at the 5 per cent level ($t = 2.07$). We may then proceed with some confidence that we do have a difference in degree of conflict.

Table 2.2 presents the data, for the four experimental conditions, on the extent to which there has been systematic re-evalua-

TABLE 2.2

*Mean Change in Attractiveness Ratings Favoring
the Chosen Alternative*
(Increase for Chosen plus Decrease for Rejected Alternative)

	High Conflict	Low Conflict
Dissonance	+1.0	+0.6
No Dissonance	+0.2	+0.3

tion of the alternatives to favor the chosen one. This measure of systematic divergence in attractiveness is simply the sum of any increase in attractiveness of the chosen alternative and any decrease in attractiveness of the rejected alternative. Positive change means that the alternatives were spread apart, negative change that they were brought closer together.

The data present a very clear pattern. In the two dissonance conditions, where the subject received only the chosen record, there is appreciable change in the direction of spreading the alternatives apart. The average change is +1.0 in the high-conflict–dissonance condition and +.6 in the low-conflict–dissonance condition. Each of these changes is significantly different from zero, $t = 4.52$ (less than the 1 per cent level) and 2.49 (less than the 5 per cent level), respectively. On the other hand, in the two no-dissonance conditions the changes are negligible (+.2 and +.3) and do not even come close to significance. Furthermore, the magnitude of the change in the dissonance conditions is significantly greater than that in the no-dissonance conditions. An analysis of variance yields an F of 5.63, which is significant at less than the 5 per cent level. None of the other F values in the analysis of variance approaches significance.

The interpretation of the data seems to be reasonably clear. If there is no dissonance created after the decision, then, irrespective of the degree of conflict during the decision, there is little or no systematic re-evaluation of the alternatives. Hence, it seems highly unlikely that such systematic re-evaluation occurs during the process of making a decision. On the other hand, when dissonance is created after the decision, there is significant re-evaluation of the alternatives for both the high- and the low-conflict conditions. Clearly, the suggested interpretation is that such systematic re-evaluation of alternatives to favor the chosen one occurs only after the decision has been made in order to reduce dissonance, and does *not* occur in the pre-decision period in order to enable the person to make the decision.

There is, of course, the interesting suggestion in the data that if the decision is preceded by high conflict, dissonance reduction after the decision may be more effective than if the decision is preceded by low conflict. The change of $+1.0$ in the high-conflict–dissonance condition is different from the change of $+0.6$ in the low-conflict–dissonance condition at about the 20 per cent level. Although this is not an impressive level of significance, the suggestion is interesting. The difference probably does not reflect any re-evaluation that may have occurred before the decision, as indicated by the results for the no-dissonance conditions. Hence, if the difference is a real one, it suggests that the greater amount of deliberation in the high-conflict condition somehow makes it easier to reduce dissonance later.

An Additional Experiment. We must ask whether the data presented in Table 2.2 are really unequivocal with respect to the indicated theoretical conclusion. The answer seems to be no, since it is still possible, although perhaps a bit difficult, to maintain an explanation of the data in terms of conflict resolution. One could maintain that, during the process of making a decision in the high-conflict condition, there is, indeed, systematic re-evaluation of the alternatives that enables the person to make the decision. In the high-conflict–no-dissonance condition, after the subject actually receives both records, this process may reverse itself, resulting in no measured over-all change. Such an explanation would also be consistent with the obtained small difference between the two dissonance conditions. In the high-conflict–dissonance condition the effects of both pre- and post-decision re-evaluation of the alternatives would have summated, resulting in a greater total change.

How can we resolve this final ambiguity of interpretation? If the results in the high-conflict–no-dissonance condition are to be explained in terms of a reversal of the re-evaluation process after the subject actually receives both records, then clearly what we need is a condition where the re-evaluation is measured after the choice has been made, but before the subject draws a slip of paper to discover whether she receives only one or both of the alternatives. In an attempt to clarify the theoretical issue further, three additional conditions were run in the experiment.

The subjects for these additional conditions were 30 girls from the same high school. Ten girls were run in each condition. Two of the conditions, high conflict and low conflict, were conducted with procedures identical to those used previously through the point of making their decision. After the decision had been made, the procedure diverged from that described. Immediately after the decision, instead of having the subject draw the slip of paper from the box, she was asked to rate each of the phonograph records a second time, using instructions identical to those in the previous experiment. Thus, for these two groups, the measure of re-evaluation of alternatives was obtained after the decision had been made but before the subject knew for certain whether she would get both records or only the record she had chosen.

Since the time interval between the decision and the measurement was, of necessity, different in these two conditions from what it was in the previous four experimental conditions, a third new condition was run to provide a basis for comparison. The procedure was identical with the others except that there was no mention of any extra records and no mention of any probability or possibility of getting both. Each girl in this condition knew that she would get only the one record she chose. Re-evaluation was again measured immediately after the decision. This condition, which we shall call the ordinary decision condition, is, of course, one in which we know from previous experiments that one does obtain systematic re-evaluation of the alternatives. Consequently, it provides a basis for evaluating the observed changes in the other two additional conditions, holding constant the time between the decision and the measurement.

Again, of course, it is necessary to look at the decision times to be sure that the manipulation of degree of conflict was successful. The mean decision time for the low-conflict condition was 7.1 seconds, for the high-conflict condition it was 10.5 seconds, and for the ordinary decision condition it was 11.7 seconds. These values are very similar to the corresponding ones in the previous experiment. The decision time for the low-conflict condition is significantly different from either the high- or the maximum-conflict condition (6 per cent and 5 per cent levels of significance,

TABLE 2.3

Mean Change in Attractiveness Ratings Before Knowing
Whether One or Both Records Will Be Obtained

Condition	Mean Change
Low Conflict	−0.1
High Conflict	−0.3
Ordinary Decision	+0.6

respectively). The high-conflict and ordinary decision conditions are, of course, not significantly different from each other.

Table 2.3 presents the data on re-evaluation of the alternatives for these three conditions. The results are clear and completely convincing. In the maximum-conflict condition the usual expected dissonance-reduction effect is obtained. There is a change of +0.6, which is significantly different from zero (2 per cent level of significance) and which is comparable in magnitude to the changes observed in the two dissonance conditions of the previous experiment. The low- and high-conflict conditions, however, show no significant changes in the evaluation of the alternatives. The actually observed changes are slightly in a negative direction. Clearly, there could have been no systematic re-evaluation of the attractiveness of the alternatives in the high-conflict condition. We can clearly and unequivocally reject the hypothesis that stems from conflict-resolution theories. The spreading apart of the attractiveness of the alternatives does *not* occur in the pre-decision period but only in the post-decision period in response to the existence of dissonance.

Summary

An experiment with seven experimental conditions was carried out in order to ascertain whether systematic re-evaluation of choice alternatives occurred before or after a decision had been made. In all conditions, high school girls were offered a choice between two phonograph records. Their ratings of the attractiveness of these records were measured both before and after the choice.

In three of the conditions low conflict was produced by telling the subjects that the probability was very high that they would get both records. In three other conditions high conflict was produced by telling the subjects that the probability was very high that they would get only the record they chose. In the seventh condition no mention was made of any possibility of getting both records, it being clearly understood that they would simply get the one they chose. In the low- and the high-conflict conditions, some subjects rerated the records after they discovered that they received both records, some after they discovered that they received only the record they chose, and some while they were still not certain whether they would get both or only one.

The results show that there is no spreading apart in the attractiveness of the alternatives if the subjects actually receive both records or if the rerating is done before they are certain of how many they will get. There is significant spreading apart of the attractiveness of the alternatives if they receive only one record, irrespective of the manipulation of the probability of getting both. It is clear that dissonance reduction, at least in this experimental situation, is entirely a post-decision phenomenon.

■

The extent to which the Davidson and Kiesler experiment and the Jecker experiment yield similar results and corroborate each other is impressive and is worth reviewing. Both experiments show significant amounts of dissonance reduction when re-evaluation of alternatives is measured after dissonance has been produced by a decision. Both experiments show that if post-decision dissonance has not been produced, there is little or no evidence of any systematic re-evaluation of the choice alternatives.

Although there are some theoretical ambiguities in interpreting the Davidson and Kiesler result by itself, these ambiguities vanish when one considers both experiments together. One may regard the theoretical question as settled. There is a clear and undeniable difference between the cognitive processes that occur during the period of making a decision and those that occur after the decision has been made. Re-evaluation of alternatives in the direction of favoring the chosen or disfavoring the rejected alternative, or both, is a post-decision phenomenon. While we have as yet cast no light on what cognitive processes do go on during the period of making a decision, we at least know that this one does not occur.

There is another point on which the two experiments corroborate each other. The reader will recall that in the Davidson and Kiesler experiment there was greater dissonance reduction after the decision when the subjects had more time to think about things in the pre-decision period. It will also be recalled that Jecker found a similar result. There was greater post-decision dissonance reduction in the condition that produced greater pre-decision conflict. In neither experiment did this difference reach very high levels of statistical significance, but the fact that the same kind of difference was obtained in two experiments that differed so radically in their design lends some weight to the result. It is at least interesting enough to warrant an attempt to understand it.

Since the evidence that spreading apart of the alternatives does not occur in the pre-decision period is very persuasive, the effect on post-decision dissonance reduction of greater time spent thinking about the alternatives, or of greater conflict between the alternatives, must be an indirect one. The following explanation, or hunch, suggests itself. The pre-decision period is probably one in which the good and bad aspects of each alternative are considered and examined impartially. The more time one has to think about the decision, or the greater the conflict, the greater is the extent to which all the various aspects have been examined. It may well be that the greater the consideration beforehand and, hence, the more detailed or elaborate the cognitions about the alternatives at the time of decision, the more rapidly or more effectively can dissonance reduction proceed. We can only leave this as a suggestion here but we shall have more to say concerning this interaction between pre- and post-decision processes in the next chapter.

One other aspect of the results is quite suggestive and requires consideration. It will be recalled that Jecker had two conditions in his experiment in which re-evaluation of alternatives was measured after the decision but before the subjects knew whether they would get both alternatives or only the one they chose. Neither of these conditions showed any dissonance reduction, the actual changes being slightly in the negative direction. These results, while fortunately persuasive with respect to the theoretical issue that was under consideration, are also rather surprising. They certainly show that systematic re-evaluation of the alternatives did not occur before the decision was made, but they also show quite conclusively that the mere fact of having made a decision is not sufficient to cause dissonance-reduction processes to begin. Let us consider the high-conflict condition to see what is implied by this result. The subjects in this condition, after having made their decision, know with certainty that they will receive the record they chose. They also know that it is very likely that they will receive only that record. They had been told that only one out of twenty subjects would be given both records.

One might have expected that under such conditions they would react almost like subjects who were faced with a simple choice in which they knew they were to get only the record they chose. But apparently the 5 per cent chance of getting both records makes a great difference. Dissonance-reduction processes do not begin until the outcomes are clear and definite. It is almost as if cognitive processes relating to re-evaluation of the alternatives were held in abeyance until the subject knew the outcome. Usually, of course, a decision has changed the situation definitely. This particular decision situation does not. Two possibilities still remain after the decision. We shall have more to say about this also in the following chapter.

Chapter Three

The Onset and Rapidity of Post-Decision Processes

■

It seems clear, in the light of the results of the experiments presented in Chapter 2, that systematic re-evaluation of alternatives does not occur prior to a decision. While all of these results point in this direction, by far the most critical and convincing evidence was produced by the final set of conditions in the experiment by Jecker. These results showed that even after a decision was made, no dissonance reduction occurred if the person was still uncertain as to whether she would get only the chosen alternative or both.

This finding, however, poses a serious problem for the theory of cognitive dissonance. This theory has, in the past, assumed that dissonance-reduction processes did not begin until after a decision had been made, and in this respect it seems to be correct. But the theory has also assumed that the making of the decision produces dissonance and that, consequently, dissonance-reduction processes *should* start once the decision is made. In this respect the theory does not seem to be entirely correct. In the Jecker experiment we find a situation in which the decision has been made but dissonance reduction does not occur. We clearly need a better understanding of the character of a decision and the conditions that determine the onset of a dissonance-reduction process.

We can make some progress in this direction by exploring some possible explanations of the Jecker result. Two such explanations come to mind quickly. One rests on the fact that when there is a possibility of obtaining both records, the subject has not clearly rejected either of the alternatives. It may be that for dissonance-reduction processes to start, it is necessary for the decision to commit the person definitely to giving something up. At least, this may be true in a situation where both alternatives have predominantly positive attributes. Thus, the commitment which ordinarily results from a decision may have been absent in the Jecker experiment.

Another possible interpretation is linked to the extent to which making a decision eliminates uncertainties in the outcome of the decision. Normally, a decision when made is a very definite thing. If a person buys a car, accepts a job, or marries a girl, the outcome of the decision is definite. He now has that particular car, job, or girl. But in the Jecker experiment a peculiar decision situation has been created. The person chooses a record but is not sure that he does not also have the other record. Perhaps dissonance reduction simply cannot begin until uncertainties are eliminated.

It seemed worthwhile to design an experiment that would explore these interpretations further and would enable us to choose between them. One could vary the degree to which there was uncertainty concerning the outcome following the decision. One could also vary, independently, whether the uncertainty did, or not not, concern the rejected alternative. Such an experiment should enable us to clarify the interpretation of the Jecker result. In addition, considering the importance of this result to the question of whether or not systematic re-evaluation of the alternatives occurs prior to the decision, it is worthwhile to see if it can be repeated. In the following pages Vernon Allen presents an experiment designed to answer these questions.

Experiment

Uncertainty of Outcome and Post-Decision Dissonance Reduction

Vernon Allen

A considerable amount of experimental evidence is now available to show that dissonance reduction does indeed occur after a decision. In addition to the results presented in Chapter 2, Festinger (1957) and Brehm and Cohen (1962) review a large amount of such data. Post-decision dissonance reduction has been observed so often that it is particularly important to demonstrate some of the conditions under which it does *not* occur. The experiment by Jecker in the preceding chapter reports such a set of conditions. Specifically, girls were given a choice between two phonograph records. If, after having made their decision they were still uncertain whether they would get just the chosen one or would get both, no post-decision dissonance reduction was observed. Furthermore, it is interesting to note in Jecker's data that the exact probability the girl perceived of getting both records seemed to be irrelevant for this result. Whether the subject was told that the chances of getting both records were only one out of 20 or were 19 out of 20 made no difference. There was no evidence of any dissonance reduction as long as any possibility of getting both records remained.

The design of the Jecker study does not allow us to judge the relative adequacy of the two possible interpretations of this result that have been discussed by Festinger in the introduction to this chapter. To test whether the absence of dissonance reduction is ascribable purely to the uncertainty of outcome, or to the fact that the particular uncertainty involved the possibility of receiving a second *desirable* alternative, requires a more elaborate design. The present experiment, designed to choose between these interpretations, stayed very close to the procedure employed by Jecker. Within this procedure, experimental conditions were created in which uncertainty of outcome was varied independently of the possibility of receiving the unchosen alternative.

Procedure

One hundred and twenty-four girls were recruited from three high schools located on the San Francisco peninsula. The girls ranged in age from 13 to 18, the mean age being 15.4 years. The subjects were recruited from study halls and were assigned randomly to one of four experimental conditions. When a "choice inversion" occurred in a condition, i.e., when a subject chose a record she had initially rated the less desirable of the two, the next subject was assigned to the same condition so that there would be about the same number of subjects in each condition who chose the initially preferred alternative.

An attempt was made to replicate the procedure of the Jecker experiment as exactly as possible. Each subject was interviewed individually. After introducing himself, the experimenter explained that he was doing some market research in order to get information about how people felt toward phonograph records that were currently popular. The experimenter also informed the subject that he was giving away some records free in exchange for her help in the research.

After a short interview designed to lend credibility to the ostensible purpose of the study, the subject was shown 15 popular phonograph records and asked to indicate, for each one, whether or not she was familiar with it, whether or not she owned it, and how much she would like to have it. For this last rating the subject used a seven-point scale on which zero was described as "don't care" and 6 was labeled "would rather have this record than any other record I can think of right now."

When these ratings had been completed, appropriate instructions were given to create the following four experimental conditions:

1. "Only Chosen" Condition. In this condition the subject was definitely to receive the record she chose and no more. The experimenter said:

As I said earlier, I'm giving away free records to people in exchange for helping in this research. Now, I have two records here. Would you tell me which one of these you would rather have?

2. "Nothing or Chosen" Condition. In this condition the subject had equal chances of getting the record she chose and getting nothing at all. The experimenter said:

As I said earlier, I'm giving away free records to people in exchange for helping in this research. Now, I can give about half the people a free record. I'm deciding randomly who will get a free record by letting people draw a slip of paper, later, from this box. There are an equal number of slips of paper in the box that have a 1 on them, and that have a zero. So you have an equal chance of getting a free record or of not getting one. Now, I have two records here. In case you get one, will you tell me which one of these you would rather have?

3. "Chosen or Both" Condition. In this condition the subject would definitely receive the record she chose and, in addition, had a 50 per cent chance of also receiving the other record. The experimenter said:

As I said earlier, I'm giving away free records to people in exchange for helping in this research. Now, I have enough records to definitely give you one, and to give about half the people two. I'm deciding randomly who will get two free records by letting people draw a slip of paper from this box. There are an equal number of slips of paper in the box that have a 1 on them, and that have a 2. So, you have an equal chance of getting one record or of getting two. Now, I have two records here. In case you get only one of these two, will you tell me which one of these you would rather have?

4. "Nothing, Chosen, or Both" Condition. In this condition the subject had equal chances of getting no records at all, of getting the one she chose, and of getting both records. The experimenter said:

As I said earlier, I'm giving away free records in exchange for helping in this research. I'm giving each person either one record, no record at all, or two records. I'm deciding randomly who will get one record, none at all, or two records by letting people draw a slip of paper, later, from this box. There are an equal number of slips of paper that have a zero, a 1, and a 2 on them. So you have an equal chance of getting a free record, of not getting one, or of getting two records. Now, I have two records here. In case you get one of these two, will you tell me which one you would rather have?

These four conditions constituted a two by two factorial design: high and low certainty of outcome of the decision, and possibility of receiving and of not receiving the unchosen record.

After the appropriate instructions had been given to the subject, the experimenter handed her two records and asked her to choose one. These two records, selected by the experimenter on the basis of the initial ratings made by the subject, had been rated either 3 and 4, or 4 and 5, on the seven-point scale. Only three of the subjects had to be discarded because they had not initially rated any two records in this manner and so could not be offered an appropriate choice.

After the subject indicated her choice between the two records, the experimenter occupied himself for two minutes on the pretext of making some notes. At the end of the two-minute period the experimenter said that he would like to have the subject's second reactions to the records. It was explained that on this second rating the subject might find she liked some records better or some less well than the first time, or she might not change her feelings about any of them. In any case, the experimenter explained, he would like to have ratings of the way she felt now. The subject then rated each of the 15 records for a second time on the same seven-point scale.

After the second rating, subjects in the appropriate conditions drew slips of paper from a box. The contents of these had been arranged so that each subject was actually given either one or two records as a free gift.

Results

We are concerned in this experiment with the relative magnitudes of dissonance reduction in the four experimental conditions, that is, with the extent to which the chosen alternative increases and the rejected alternative decreases in attractiveness after the decision. If the degree of uncertainty of outcome is the primary factor determining the onset of dissonance reduction, then the subjects in the nothing-or-chosen condition should show less dissonance reduction than those in the only-chosen condition. Subjects in the "nothing, chosen, or both" condition should likewise show less than those in the chosen-or-both condition. On the other hand, if the possibility of receiving both alternatives is the determining factor, then the absence of dissonance reduction should be observed equally in the chosen-or-both and the "nothing, chosen, or both" conditions. Of course, both factors might operate simultaneously. If so, the data would show this.

Before presenting the results, however, we must deal with a methodological problem. Of the 121 subjects from whom usable data were collected, 24 chose the record that they had originally rated as the *less* desirable of the two. This was a surprise to us, since in the original Jecker experiment this problem did not exist, and we had attempted to replicate the Jecker procedure as closely as possible. The data from these 24 subjects cannot, of course, be combined with the other data. We will, consequently, present the results separately for the 97 subjects whose choice was consistent with their initial ratings and then, later, will present the results for the other 24 subjects. It will be seen, however, that the variation among the conditions in the number of "decision inversions" cannot account for any of the obtained differences.

Table 3.1 presents the data on the change from pre-decision to post-decision rating for the chosen and the unchosen alternative separately. The data are presented separately here because, in this experiment, in contrast to the usual finding, differential changes occurred only with respect to the rejected alternative. In all cases a plus sign indicates change in the direction of dissonance reduction.

It is clear from examining Table 3.1 that there are no differences of any importance among the conditions on change in the desirability of the chosen alternative. All the conditions change somewhat in the positive direction. Considering that subjects in each condition were deleted from the analysis because of "decision inversions," there is little one can say about the absolute magnitude of dissonance reduction. The only thing we can say is that there are no differences among the conditions.

Table 3.1, however, shows a very different picture concerning the changes in desirability of the unchosen alternative. Here it is quite clear that when there is a possibility of receiving both alternatives, there is no change in the desirability of the unchosen one. When it is impossible to obtain both, when the decision has committed the person to give up something, then the unchosen alternative becomes less desirable. An analysis of variance shows the dif-

TABLE 3.1

Changes from Pre-Decision to Post-Decision Ratings in the Direction of Dissonance Reduction

Possibility of Obtaining Both Alternatives	Certainty of Outcome	
	More Certain	Less Certain
The Chosen Alternative:		
Impossible	+.28	+.20
Possible	+.21	+.29
The Unchosen Alternative:		
Impossible	+.28	+.32
Possible	−.04	+.04

NOTE: Number of cases (N) in the experimental conditions:
Impossible–More Certain ("Only Chosen"), N = 25
Impossible–Less Certain ("Nothing or Chosen"), N = 25
Possible–More Certain ("Chosen or Both"), N = 23
Possible–Less Certain ("Nothing, Chosen, or Both"), N = 24

ference between the "both possible" and the "both impossible" conditions to be close to an acceptable level of significance, $F = 3.16$, which is significant at the 8 per cent level. The reduction in desirability of the unchosen alternative in the "impossible" conditions is significantly different from zero at less than the 1 per cent level.

The data are, then, clear with respect to the two possible interpretations of the Jecker result that we had in mind in designing this experiment. Variation in the degree of uncertainty of outcome has no effect on the onset of dissonance reduction. The possibility of obtaining both alternatives is the important variable. In this situation the subjects do reduce dissonance if the decision commits them to give up the unchosen alternative. Incidentally, it is worth pointing out that the Jecker result is well confirmed here. In the chosen-or-both condition there was no dissonance reduction.

Let us now turn our attention to the 24 subjects who chose the alternative that they had initially rated as the less desirable. Actually, these "decision inversions" are almost non-existent in two of the four conditions. In the only-chosen and in the chosen-or-both conditions, the two conditions that were similar to those run in the Jecker experiment, there are very few such "inversions"—only two in each. In the nothing-or-chosen and in the "nothing, chosen, or both" conditions, on the other hand, there are 11 and 9 "decision inversions," respectively. Indeed, it seems that the possibility of obtaining no free record at all induced a large number of "decision inversions." The differences are, of course, highly significant. Why this should have such an effect is not clear. Perhaps there are some people who feel that if they ask for less, then fate will be kind to them. At any rate, it is clear that the number of "decision inversions" that were excluded from the analysis cannot account for the results we obtained. Indeed, there is no relationship at all between the number of "decision inversions" and the amount of dissonance reduction among the four conditions.

With the small number of cases in two of the conditions, it makes little sense to examine the dissonance-reduction data for these 24 subjects separately for each experimental condition. Table 3.2, consequently, presents these data combining those two conditions in which it was not possible to obtain both alternatives

TABLE 3.2

Changes from Pre-Decision to Post-Decision Ratings for
Those Subjects Who Chose the Less Desirable Alternative

Condition	N	Alternative	
		Chosen	Unchosen
Only One Alternative Possible	13	+ .8	+.8
Both Alternatives Possible	11	+1.0	+.3

NOTE: A positive sign indicates change in the direction of dissonance reduction.

and combining those two conditions in which it *was* possible to obtain both. The absolute level of change for these subjects does not have much meaning. We can, however, compare the two sets of conditions. It is interesting to note that the difference is in the same direction as for the other subjects. The major difference between the two sets of conditions is in the change in attractiveness of the unchosen alternative. There is appreciable change only when it is impossible to obtain both alternatives. With such a small number of cases, and with considerable variability, this difference does not approach an acceptable level of significance. We present it merely to show that the dissonance-reduction results for these 24 subjects exhibit the same pattern that we found in the main analysis of the data.

Summary

An experiment was performed to clarify the interpretation of a finding by Jecker that after a decision there was no dissonance reduction if the person was still uncertain whether she was to obtain only the alternative chosen or both alternatives. Four different experimental conditions were run, each involving a different possible outcome following the decision. In one condition the subject was definitely to receive the chosen alternative and nothing more; in another condition she had an equal chance of receiving the chosen alternative or receiving nothing; a third condition provided an equal chance of receiving only the chosen alternative or receiving both; and a fourth condition provided equal chances of nothing, the chosen alternative, or both alternatives.

The results showed that the degree of uncertainty concerning the outcome of the decision did not affect the onset of the process of dissonance reduction. The important factor was clearly whether or not there was a possibility of obtaining both alternatives. If such a possibility existed, there was no significant dissonance reduction. If there was no such possibility, dissonance reduction was observed.

■

It would seem from the results of the study reported by Allen that we can now say something of a generalizable nature about factors determining the onset of dissonance reduction.

We must accept the fact that dissonance-reduction processes do not automatically start when a decision is made. After all, the Jecker finding was replicated. Following a decision, there is no dissonance reduction if the possibility of obtaining both alternatives still exists. If we recall that in one of the conditions of Jecker's experiment this possibility was only one chance in twenty, it is clear that simply making a decision is not enough. The decision must have the effect of committing the person. As long as it is not definite that the unchosen alternative is rejected, the decision has not committed the person.

It turns out that for purposes of distinguishing between pre-decision and post-decision processes, Jecker was fortunate in hitting on a condition in which dissonance reduction did not occur. The replication of Jecker's result helps make it very clear that systematic re-evaluation of the alternatives does not take place prior to a decision.

Let us, then, turn our attention to the other suggestion arising from the experiments reported in Chapter 2. What are the possible effects of the pre-decision processes on the dissonance reduction that does occur following the decision? That there may be an effect is suggested by the persistent result (persistent through two studies) that greater dissonance reduction is obtained after a decision if the person has spent more time in the pre-decision period considering the alternatives.

We must emphasize at this point, however, that on the basis of the results presented in Chapter 2 this is merely a suggestion.

Neither in the Davidson and Kiesler experiment nor in the Jecker experiment did the result approach a level of statistical significance that would give us very much confidence in it. Furthermore, it perhaps requires a slight stretch of the imagination to see the results of those two studies as the same in this regard. In one study deliberation time was specifically manipulated. In the other, magnitude of conflict was manipulated, affecting decision time, it is true, but perhaps affecting other things as well. Nevertheless, the suggestion seems well worth pursuing because, if true, it is very interesting from a theoretical point of view.

If such a result holds, how could we account for it theoretically? There is one plausible explanation that is rather uninteresting. Perhaps if a person is rushed into making a decision that he is not ready to make, or if he pays little or no attention to the decision because he thinks he will get both alternatives anyway, he subsequently feels little responsibility for the decision, experiences less dissonance, and hence reduces less dissonance. Certainly, in the Davidson and Kiesler experiment the subjects in the short-deliberation-time conditions may have felt rushed into a decision. Likewise, in the Jecker experiment, the subjects in the low-conflict condition may have felt quite sure (19 out of 20 chances) that they would get both alternatives.

There is, however, another possible explanation that is much more interesting. Let us consider the specifics of the cognitive process by means of which, in order to reduce post-decision dissonance, the person systematically re-evaluates the alternatives. It seems unlikely that this re-evaluation occurs immediately and automatically, without consideration and thought. Probably it requires some detailed consideration of specific aspects of the alternatives and re-assessment of the relative merits of the specific pros and cons. Thus, for example, a person who has just decided to buy a certain house does not tell himself simply that the house he bought is wonderful. Rather, he considers various aspects of it—its location, the neighbors, the room arrangement, its distance from where he works, and the like. These details can be re-evaluated in order to reduce the dissonance. The new house is close to where he works and he realizes that he has really become very tired of commuting; the price of the house was very high but he now sees that it can also be considered a good financial investment.

In other words, we are suggesting that dissonance reduction takes time and takes work. The interesting aspect of this suggestion is that, to some limited extent at least, it may make no difference when this work is done—before or after the decision. If the person has spent time and effort considering specific details about the alternatives before the decision, then dissonance reduction may proceed rapidly. If he has not done so before the decision, then perhaps he must spend the time to do it afterward, and hence dissonance reduction proceeds more slowly. In short, we are suggesting that in order to reduce post-decision dissonance the person must at some time engage in a process of thinking through the specific details of the alternatives. If he has done this in the pre-decision period, he need not do it afterward.

This explanation of the unexpected results of the Davidson and Kiesler and the Jecker experiments, if correct, casts some additional light on the cognitive processes involved in dissonance reduction. It is necessary, however, to be sure that the result is real and replicable. It is also necessary to produce the result under experimental conditions that render alternative explanations less plausible. In particular, we should like to have an experimental situation in which we were reasonably certain that variation in the amount of pre-dissonance consideration of information does not affect the seriousness with which the person makes the decision or the importance he attributes to the decision. One could then, conceivably, rule out the alternative explanation which assumed that greater time spent in the pre-decision period resulted in more post-decision dissonance.

The requirements for a proper experimental test of this theoretical suggestion are reasonably clear. We must be able to manipulate experimentally the degree to which the person familiarizes himself with and considers specific details that are relevant to dissonance reduction. We must do so, however, in a manner that does not provide differential inputs of information in different conditions, does not affect the seriousness of the decision, and does not affect what the person chooses to do. Perhaps the best way to do this is to vary the pre-decision deliberation time before the person even knows that there is a decision to be made.

It would be desirable, in addition, to vary the time between the occurrence of the decision and the measurement of the extent to which dissonance was reduced. In this way one could see whether pre-dissonance familiarization with details affects either the speed with which dissonance is reduced or the over-all amount of dissonance reduction. Thus, we are led to a design in which there would be two degrees of pre-decision opportunity and two degrees of post-decision opportunity to consider details. From such a design we should be able to ascertain whether or not our hunch is correct. If amount of time spent thinking about details in the pre-decision period can be substituted for time spent similarly in the post-decision period, it would be apparent in the results. An experiment designed to fulfill these requirements is reported below by Davidson.

Experiment

Cognitive Familiarity and Dissonance Reduction

Jon R. Davidson

This experiment is an attempt to test directly a hypothesis concerning the contribution that pre-decision processes may make to post-decision dissonance reduction. Considering the results of the experiments reported by Davidson and Kiesler and by Jecker in Chapter 2, it seems plausible to reason that since there is no systematic re-evaluation of alternatives prior to the decision, the pre-decision process must be largely concerned with the impartial accumulation and consideration of information about all the alternatives. Perhaps, then, it is this very accumulation of information in the pre-decision period that later serves to facilitate dissonance reduction.

It is not immediately apparent how we may test this hypothesis decisively. In the usual kind of decision situation, where a person must choose between two or more alternatives, the manipulation of pre-decision familiarity with the alternatives may affect other things as well. The decision may become more important or the person may accept more responsibility for the decision; it may even affect what the person decides. Clearly, it is desirable to have an experimental situation in which the manipulation of pre-decision thinking time would be very unlikely to have any of these side effects.

These requirements can be more closely approximated if, instead of using the usual type of decision situation for this experiment, we employ a situation that has been called, perhaps somewhat erroneously, a "forced compliance" situation. This is a situation in which the person must choose between engaging and not engaging in a given action, his freedom to choose is stressed, but the situation is arranged so that the person always decides to engage in the action.

The specific experimental situation we employed was suggested by an experiment reported by Davis and Jones (1960). In that experiment dissonance was produced by inducing subjects to utter negative evaluations of a person toward whom they actually felt rather favorably. The present experiment is closely modeled after their procedure. This situation has certain definite advantages for our purpose. First, one can plausibly vary the amount of time the subject spends thinking about the other person before the subject knows that he will be asked to read a prepared negative evaluation. Thus, pre-decision familiarity can be manipulated before the subject even knows that a decision is to be made. Second, the experimenter in this situation can control which decision is made, since the context is arranged so that all subjects decide to read the negative evaluation. The manipulation of pre-decision familiarity cannot, hence, affect the direction of the decision. Third, once the subject is asked to make the decision, no restrictions need be put on how much time he takes to decide. It seems unlikely, then, that there would be differences among conditions in the seriousness or importance of the decision for the subject, since no subjects would be rushed into making a quick decision.

Procedure

The subjects used in the experiment were male high school juniors and seniors. Sixty-six of the subjects were recruited on a volunteer basis from the Palo Alto High School and were paid $2.00 per hour for participating in the experiment. Sixteen additional subjects volunteered for the experiment from a high school honors group studying at Stanford University during the summer session. These latter subjects were not paid. Thus, a total of 82 subjects were run in the experiment. The data from six subjects were discarded. Two subjects accurately guessed that they were listening to a tape recording when they were supposedly listening to another subject being interviewed. This made their data meaningless. Four other subjects, while listening to the supposed other subject being interviewed, spontaneously expressed extreme dislike for him. Data from these subjects were discarded because reading a negative evaluation would not create dissonance for them. The 76 subjects whose data were usable were divided evenly among four experimental conditions, 19 subjects in each.

Each subject who had volunteered to participate in the experiment was contacted by telephone to arrange a specific appointment. At this time he was told that two persons were scheduled simultaneously for the experiment. When the subject arrived at the laboratory, he was seated in a small room adjacent to a larger one and was told that the other subject was already in the larger room. The two rooms were connected by a one-way mirror over which a curtain was drawn. The subject was reminded that the experiment was concerned with how people form impressions of others and that, in this particular study, we wanted to eliminate all visual cues so that we could more accurately study how impressions were formed on the basis of just listening to the other person.

The subject was further told that the two rooms were connected for sound transmission and that he would soon have the opportunity to listen to the other subject being interviewed by a professor in the adjacent room. On the subject's desk in his own small room were a set of earphones, and a microphone that clearly was not connected to the equipment in the room. This equipment, all visible, consisted of a set of dual amplifiers, a relay box with connecting wires, and two large input cords ostensibly coming to the amplifiers from the adjacent room. Partially hidden from the subject's view was a tape recorder.

The experimenter told the subject that the other person was at the moment finishing some personality questionnaires and that soon the interview in the other room would start. Actually, there was nobody in the adjacent room. The experimenter, after informing the subject that he was going to tape-record the interview, started the tape recorder and asked the subject to put on the ear-phones that ostensibly allowed him to hear what went on in the other room. The subject then heard some paper rustling and, after a short while, heard the subject in the other room say that he guessed he was finished with the questionnaire. He then heard the professor in the other room say that was fine and that as soon as he received a signal from the small room he would begin the inter-view. The tape recording went on with the fictitious professor ex-plaining to the fictitious subject that another person was in the smaller room and would be listening to the interview.

The tape recording was arranged with appropriate pauses so that an illusion of interaction between the experimenter and the fictitious professor was created. Finally, they agreed that they were ready and the interview proceeded. The fictitious subject, "Bill," was made to appear to be rather bright, well-rounded, athletically inclined, and seriously interested in science. The intention was to have him be moderately well liked by our subjects.

When the fictitious interview was concluded, the experimenter asked the subject to remove the earphones and gave him a short questionnaire to fill out. This questionnaire was the means of manipulating the amount of time the subject spent thinking about "Bill." The questionnaire consisted of 16 items that asked for judgments about whether there was a tendency for introversion or extroversion, dominance or submissiveness, preference for music or for art, and the like. In order to create a condition in which, before any decision, the subject had spent time thinking about the characteristics of the other person (high pre-decision familiarity), the experimenter introduced the questionnaire as follows:

Before we proceed any further, I'd like you to fill out this short person-ality form on which we ask you to consider and assess some personality characteristics which would best describe the other subject. Please be honest in your responses, work carefully, and answer all of the items. If a particular item seems difficult to answer, consider all you know about the other subject and make a best guess. It should take only about five minutes.

In other words, in the condition of high pre-decision familiarity the subject spent time, at this point, in considering what the other subject was like and in answering questions about him. Thus, before any decision had been made, before any dissonance had been introduced, indeed, before the subject had any idea that there was to be any decision, he had considered details about the other person.

In order to create a condition of low pre-decision familiarity holding the procedure as constant as possible otherwise, the experimenter gave the same introduction to the questionnaire except that the words "the other subject" were replaced by the word "yourself." The questionnaire that subjects in this condition were asked to fill out was also the same, except that words like "he" were replaced by words like "I." In short, in the condition of low pre-decision familiarity the subject engaged in the same task but, instead of thinking about the other subject, spent the same amount of time thinking about himself.

When this questionnaire had been completed, the experimenter proceeded to explain the rest of the experiment to the subject. The purpose of this next stage of the procedure was to induce each subject to read a derogatory, highly critical evaluation of "Bill," thinking that his words were being listened to by "Bill" who was still in the adjacent room. The attempt was made to have each subject perceive that he was really free to choose whether or not he would read the negative evaluation. In order to accomplish this, the experimenter said:

Now we proceed to the second phase of this study. We're interested not only in your impressions, but also in the reactions of the *other* subject to your opinions and evaluations of him. However, instead of having you talk to him and tell him directly and in your own words how you'd evaluate him and judge his personality, we'd like you to read an evaluation which we have already prepared.

The design of this study calls for 100 pairs of subjects, 100 in this room, and 100 in the adjacent room. Now we want to make sure that *each* subject in the other room hears precisely the *same* evaluation, so that we can study the effects of that evaluation on his behavior in a more systematic manner. If we didn't ask subjects in this room to read an evaluation we had already prepared, it would all be chaos. Do you see the point?

Now, as a matter of fact, we have two evaluations and you can choose which one you'd rather read. One is positive or complimentary in nature, while the other is negative or critical in nature. And it's our policy to let subjects choose the evaluation they'd rather read. They're of equal length. The reason we have two evaluations, positive and negative, is so that we can directly compare the effects of positive and negative evaluations on

the other subject's behavior. Uh, I might add that thus far we've run some
52 pairs of subjects and, well, quite understandably, we've had 46 cases
where the subject has chosen to read the positive evaluation.

Now, uh, you know, you can read whichever one you'd want to, though
I would kind of appreciate it, because we're trying to get an equal number of subjects in each condition, positive and negative, if you'd read the
negative one . . .

[*Experimenter waits for assent; if it is not forthcoming, he repeats the
essence of the last few sentences. Questions about the nature of the evaluations are dismissed, cordially, by stating that we're not supposed to let the
subjects read the material before their "performance" because, among
other reasons, it made the subsequent "reading" over the microphone
sound too artificial.*]

I might add that at no point during or after the study will you be able
to meet the other subject. You see, he's volunteered for a longer time
period than you, and has undergone and will undergo rather extensive
personality and behavioral tests. Also, we'll want him back at a later date
for further testing. So, I'm afraid any meeting would be impractical from
our point of view.

This procedure was reasonably successful in giving the subjects
the illusion that they had a real choice while at the same time
inducing them to read the negative evaluation. Only three subjects
showed great resistance to the idea of reading it, and all subjects
finally agreed to do so.

After the subject had indicated his willingness to read the critical evaluation of "Bill," the experimenter plugged in the microphone, handed it to the subject and asked him to read, as naturally
and convincingly as possible, the following:

Well, as I understand it, my job is to tell you in all honesty what my first
impression of you was, so here goes. I hope what I have to say won't cause
any hard feelings, but I've got to say right away that my over-all impression of you was not too favorable. To put it simply, I don't think I'd go
out of my way to meet you. Maybe I'd change my mind if we could meet
together in a more natural situation, but from what you said, and the
way that you said it, I'd guess that you have some personal problems that
would make it difficult for us to get along very well. And I got the impression that you were kind of conceited and cocky, and that kind of person
doesn't appeal to me at all.

To be more specific, it sounded as if you could only like people who
were just like you in most respects, and that kind of strikes me as being
pretty shallow and pretty, well, conceited. The kind of people you like
strikes me as being just a particular type, and kind of shallow at that.

And I got the feeling that you were more interested in making a good impression rather than being honest about yourself and your feelings.

I suppose I could point out some of the things that made a favorable impression on me, but that would be kind of a waste of time since the over-all impression I got was not too good. I guess that's all I have to say. Again, I hope there are no hard feelings, but I've got to be honest about my impressions.

The reading of this negative evaluation to the "other person" essentially concluded all the experimental manipulations, except for variation in how soon afterward a measure reflecting dissonance reduction was obtained. Half of the subjects in each familiarity condition were measured immediately while the other half were measured after an appreciable delay. In the immediate-measurement condition, questionnaires designed to measure how much the subject liked the other person were administered as quickly as feasible after the reading of the negative evaluation. In the delayed-measurement condition there were eight minutes of interpolated activity before the subject was asked to fill out the same questionnaire. The interpolated activity was designed to encourage the subject to think about the other person without giving him any actual additional information. Specifically, the subjects in the delayed-measurement condition were asked to write a short (about two-minute) "guess" about the physical characteristics of the other person, and a somewhat longer (about six-minute) summary and evaluation of the personality of the other person.

The questionnaires that were administered to measure the amount of dissonance reduction contained:

1. Three questions that directly measured the subject's liking for and attraction to the other person;

2. Two sociometric-type questions that were concerned with the subject's inclination to associate with the other person in specific activities;

3. A questionnaire that asked the subject to check on a list those specific personality characteristics that the other person possessed;

4. A series of questions designed to measure possible alternative methods of dissonance reduction, such as degree of perceived choice and perceived importance of the experiment to science.

When these questionnaires had been completed, the experiment was over. The experimenter then paid the subject (those recruited from the Palo Alto High School) and explained the true nature of the study and the reasons for the various deceptions. The subjects were, of course, asked not to divulge this information to others.

Results

Before looking at the data, a review of the design of the experiment and the theoretical expectations concerning the results may be helpful. Each subject in the experiment made a decision to read a negative evaluation to another person whom he did not really dislike, and actually proceeded to perform this action. If the subjects felt that they had really been forced to do this, little dissonance would have been generated. An attempt was made, however, to have them feel that they had a real choice in the matter. This attempt was probably successful. On the final questionnaire each subject was asked to indicate on a scale from 0 to 100 how much free choice he felt he had in deciding whether or not to read the derogatory evaluation. Zero indicated no choice at all, and 100 indicated complete freedom of choice. The average rating for all conditions combined was 60.4. In other words, on the average, the subjects felt that they had more than a moderate amount of choice in the situation.

In this experiment, dissonance was created between the subject's knowledge that he had told the other person he disliked him and the subject's own private evaluation of the other person. The major, and most direct, means of reducing this dissonance would be to change his own evaluation in a negative direction. If he could persuade himself that he really disliked the other person, there would be no dissonance. Thus, more effective dissonance reduction in this situation would be reflected by greater dislike of the other person.

The data from the four experimental conditions that were run should provide the answers to two questions. First, does dissonance reduction require that time be spent thinking about the other person; and second, is time spent before the decision substitutable for time spent after the dissonance has already been generated? There is one experimental condition in which subjects had little time to think specifically about the other person either before or after the dissonance was generated. In another condition the subjects were encouraged to think about the other person *both* before and after the decision. In one of the two remaining conditions the subjects could think about the other person before, but not after, the decision, and in the last condition this was reversed.

Let us first examine the data obtained on the three questions designed to measure general liking for the other person. Specifically, these questions asked the subjects to complete the following statements:

1. I would be happiest if he were: (six-point scale ranging from "my best friend" to "a person I did not know");

2. This person has the kind of personality that: (five-point scale ranging from "attracts me very much" to "repels me very much");

3. I like this person: (five-point scale ranging from "very, very much" to "not at all").

All of the items were scored so that a larger number indicated a greater degree of liking, with 5 being the maximum score on each question. Thus, the highest "liking score" would be 15. A subject who marked each scale in the middle would have received a score of 8.5. This would reflect his having indicated that he would be happiest if the other person was between a close friend and a classmate, that the other person neither attracts nor repels him, and that he likes the other person a fair amount. In other words, a score of 8 or 9 still represents an attitude on the positive side of the neutral point.

Table 3.3 presents the average rating of attractiveness of the other person for each of the four experimental conditions. A glance at the table shows that three of the experimental conditions yield means that are very close to one another. One of the conditions, low pre-decision familiarity–immediate measurement, is considerably different from the others. The subjects in this condition like the other person considerably better, on the average, than subjects in any of the other conditions. An analysis of variance confirms that this difference is highly significant. Although the variances based on both sets of marginal means are significant at the 5 per cent level, it is clear that the significance is entirely attributable to the greater liking in one condition. Indeed, the interaction variance yields an F of 14.1, a value that is highly significant.

As one might expect, separate t tests reveal that the mean of

TABLE 3.3

Mean Ratings of Attractiveness of the Other Person

Time of Measurement	Pre-Decision Familiarity	
	Low	High
Immediate	10.95	8.52
Delayed	8.53	9.21

NOTE: The larger the number, the greater the rated attractiveness.

10.95 for the low-familiarity–immediate-measurement condition is significantly different from each of the other means at levels better than 1 per cent. None of the other differences approaches significance.

What can be said, then, about these data? First, it seems reasonable to accept the fact that the other person was perceived initially as a rather attractive person. In the condition in which there was little time, either before or after the decision, to think about the other person, the average rating is almost 11. Since the maximum possible rating was 15, it is clear that this does represent a perception that the other person is rather attractive and likable. This condition is, of course, the one that would be expected to produce the smallest amount of dissonance reduction, and therefore it seems reasonable to accept this value as closest to the initial perception of the other person.

In the other three experimental conditions, in which subjects spent time thinking about the other person before the decision, after the decision, or both, there is considerably more dissonance reduction in the direction of actually becoming less favorably inclined toward the other person. Comparing the mean for the condition that permitted thinking time before the decision and not afterward with the mean for the condition that permitted thinking time afterward but not before, we find that these means are almost identical, both about 8.5. Clearly, time spent thinking about details of the other person before the decision (before they even knew there was to be a decision) does actually facilitate post-decision dissonance reduction and does, indeed, seem to be substitutable for time spent after the dissonance already exists.

It is profitable at this point to consider a question of interpretation. Can we be confident that the obtained differences among

the conditions are due to different amounts of dissonance reduction, or could they have arisen for other plausible reasons? Some
might argue, for example, that by some mischance the recorded
interview created an image of the other person that was superfi-
cially likable, but that the more one thought about him, the more
one realized that he was not likable. How can one refute this kind
of alternative explanation?

One way to show that the results are really due to the effects of
dissonance reduction, and not to something else, is to show that
the measure of dissonance reduction, namely, how much the subjects like the other person, is related to other variables that we
know would affect the magnitude of dissonance. It will be recalled
that in the process of inducing the subjects to read the negative
evaluation, the attempt was made to have them perceive a high
degree of choice. This attempt was reasonably successful but, of
course, not uniformly so. There was considerable variability in
how much free choice the subjects perceived they had. One may
reason that the less free choice they felt they had, the less dissonance was created and, consequently, the smaller the amount of
dissonance reduction should be. Thus, if the results are really
due to a dissonance-reduction process, we would expect to find a
negative relation between the amount of perceived choice and how
well they like the other person. Such negative correlations do exist
for each of the four experimental conditions. They range from
$-.19$ to $-.42$, with an average correlation of $-.32$ that is significant at better than the 5 per cent level.

There is, thus, some evidence that the effects are due to a dissonance-reduction process. However, evidence from such internal
correlations is never wholly satisfactory. It might be contended,
for example, that those subjects who initially liked the other person better showed more resistance when the experimenter asked
them to read the negative evaluation. The experimenter may then
have exerted more pressure on them, and their perception of
having had less free choice may indeed be a veridical one.

In order to settle this question unequivocally it is really necessary to show that, in the absence of the introduction of any dissonance, time spent thinking about details concerning the other
person does not have any effect in and of itself. Consequently, two
additional groups of subjects were run. These subjects were all

male students recruited from the Palo Alto High School and paid for participating. The procedure for one group was the same as that for the condition of low pre-decision familiarity; for the other, it was the same as that for the condition of high pre-decision familiarity, up to the point where, in the original experiment, subjects were asked to read the negative evaluation. But these two additional groups of subjects never had any dissonance created. After the familiarity manipulation, they were simply asked to answer the final questionnaire.

Ten subjects were run in each of these control conditions. The results are very clear. The average attractiveness of the other person is 10.0 for the low-familiarity control condition and 11.2 for the high-familiarity control condition. Clearly, the familiarity manipulation, in and of itself, does not reduce the liking for the other person. In fact, the difference is in the opposite direction and is statistically significant (5 per cent level). It does seem that the familiarity questionnaire did not induce subjects to view "Bill" as less attractive but, if anything, made them see him as more attractive. We may, thus, be confident that the differences in Table 3.3 are attributable to the effects of dissonance reduction.

Let us return, then, to the data presented in Table 3.3. The results for the condition in which the subjects were given thinking time both before and after the dissonance was created present a bit of a problem. The subjects in this condition, having had high pre-decision familiarity with the other person, should have been able to reduce dissonance immediately after the dissonance was generated just as in the high-familiarity–immediate-measurement condition. Given the additional time to reduce dissonance further after having read the negative evaluation, one might expect them to show the greatest amount of dissonance reduction. However, they do not. They reduce no more dissonance than subjects in the conditions that permitted thinking time only before or only after reading the negative evaluation. Indeed, there is a slight difference in the data in the opposite direction from what would be expected.

How can this rather puzzling result be explained? It may be that there is a real limit to the degree to which a person can persuade himself that a likable other is really not likable, and perhaps this limit has been reached. But if this is the case, one may still ask what the subjects who were permitted thinking time both before and after the decision were doing in the time interval after the

decision. If, immediately after having read the negative evaluation, they have already reduced as much dissonance as they reasonably can in the direction of persuading themselves that the other
person is not really likeable, what, if anything, do they do during
the ensuing delay? One possibility, of course, is that they utilize
this extra time to reduce dissonance along other avenues. Perhaps
they are more successful in distorting the other person's actual
characteristics; perhaps they persuade themselves more that the
experiment is important for science. Let us then proceed to look
at the results we obtained concerning these other avenues of dissonance reduction.

At the end of the experimental session, three questions were
asked that were designed to check on other possible means of
reducing dissonance. It is theoretically possible for subjects to have
further justified having read the negative evaluation to the other
person by persuading themselves that they had really had little
choice in the matter, that the experimenter had virtually forced
them to do it, that the experiment was very important for science—
certainly a good reason for doing it—and that they had enjoyed
helping the experimenter in a scientific experiment. Accordingly,
the subjects were asked to indicate on scales going from zero to 100
how much choice they felt they had in deciding which evaluation
to read, how important they thought the experiment was, and
how much they enjoyed participating in it.

The question on perceived degree of choice produced nothing
but trivial differences among the conditions. The other two questions, however, produced differences that, although far from being
statistically significant, nevertheless are suggestive. Table 3.4 pre-

TABLE 3.4

*Average Ratings of Importance of Experiment
and Enjoyment of Participation*

Time of Measurement	Pre-Decision Familiarity			
	Importance		Enjoyment	
	Low	High	Low	High
Immediate	64.2	64.7	82.1	86.0
Delayed	64.7	74.7	79.7	90.8

NOTE: A larger number indicates greater importance and more enjoyment.

sents the means on these two questions for the four experimental conditions. It is clear that on each of these two questions there is a tendency for greater dissonance reduction to have occurred in the high-familiarity–delayed-measurement condition. The subjects in that condition perceived the experiment as somewhat more important and also tended to enjoy it more. The point should not be belabored since the differences are far from significant statistically, but there is some suggestion that the subjects in the high-familiarity–delayed-measurement condition may have reduced additional dissonance in ways other than by derogating the other person.

The reader will recall that several questions attempted to measure the subjects' perception of specific personality characteristics of the other person. Two of these were questions of the sociometric type, which asked about willingness to participate with the other person in an intellectual activity and in a recreational activity. The other questions were in the form of a "personality inventory" on which the subject was asked to choose between favorable and unfavorable personality characteristics to describe the other person. It might have been expected that dissonance reduction in the direction of liking the other person less would also have been reflected in the attributes and personality characteristics which he was seen to possess. This, however, turned out not to be the case. The differences among the four experimental conditions on these questions were entirely negligible.

This rather surprising finding calls for some thought. Differences of rather large magnitude in the over-all evaluation of how much they like the other person are not paralleled by differences in the traits and characteristics which they perceive the other person possesses. Apparently, we must assert that the subjects in this situation do not reduce dissonance by distorting their perception of the specific characteristics the other person possesses. They reduce dissonance rather by changing their opinions and evaluations of those characteristics or combinations of characteristics.

Summary

An experiment was carried out to test whether or not thinking about details relevant to future dissonance reduction would facilitate dissonance reduction even though the thinking was done before any dissonance had been introduced or anticipated.

Using a procedure very similar to that employed by Davis and Jones (1960), subjects were induced to express negative evaluations of and to another person whom they initially liked. The amount of dissonance reduction was measured primarily by the extent to which, afterward, they disliked this other person.

Four experimental conditions were employed in a factorial design that varied the amount of time the subjects were permitted to think about the other person either before or after dissonance was created. The results indicate that increased familiarity before dissonance is created does indeed facilitate the reduction of dissonance afterward.

■

The Davidson experiment, by and large, confirms the theoretical hunch stemming from the experiments reported in Chapter 2. The process of dissonance reduction does, indeed, require that time be spent in thinking about the characteristics of the alternatives. If such detailed cognitive familiarity is acquired before a decision, dissonance reduction seems to proceed more quickly because the person does not have to spend comparable time afterward to acquire that cognitive familiarity. Thus, although systematic reevaluation of alternatives does not occur in the pre-decision period, the accumulation of, and consideration of, information in that period does have an impact on post-decision dissonance reduction.

If one speculates further about the results of the Davidson experiment, there is the interesting suggestion that the dissonance-reduction process is not one of distortion, but mainly one of reevaluation in that experimental situation. It will be remembered that there was not even any hint of differences among conditions in the subjects' perception of the specific personality characteristics that the other person had. We are almost forced to the conclusion, then, that under some circumstances the process of reducing dissonance depends primarily on changing one's evaluation of the specific aspects that one knows to exist. Thus, for example, if a person is seen as being very intelligent and also a good athlete, one could persuade oneself that intelligence is not really important in evaluating how likable a person is, or that there is probably something wrong with a person who tries so hard to be good at everything. Of course, it is quite possible that in extreme instances actual distortion of one's perception may occur. In this experiment, at least, there was no evidence for this.

Chapter Four

Seeking Information Before and After Decisions

■

In the preceding chapters we have presented evidence that the cognitive processes before and after decisions differ strikingly from each other. After a decision, these processes enhance the attractiveness of the chosen alternative and reduce the attractiveness of the rejected alternative. We found that such divergence in the attractiveness of the alternatives did not occur during the pre-decision period. The cognitive processes must, indeed, be different during these two periods in order to produce such different end results.

If these processes are so different, one should be able to obtain direct evidence that describes the differences between them. One should be able to observe that before a decision is made, for example, the person pays equal amounts of attention to both alternatives, and that his evaluation of information about each alternative is equally objective. After a decision one should observe a lack of objectivity in a direction supporting the choice. If, under well-controlled conditions, one could obtain direct measurements which described the two cognitive processes, this would add greatly to the weight of our interpretations.

Measurement of the details of an ongoing cognitive process is never easy to accomplish, however. It seems plausible to suppose that if we want to know what is going on in the mind of a person, all we have to do is ask him the appropriate questions at the appropriate times. If, for example, one wants to know whether a person is appraising a piece of information critically or favorably, one can simply interrupt the person while he is in the process of considering the information, and ask him how he has been viewing it and what his thought processes were. Such a procedure, however, rarely proves to be feasible in practice. The data obtained in this manner are of doubtful validity. There are two major reasons for this. First, it is difficult, if not impossible, to ask meaningful questions without putting thoughts into the person's cognition, or into his mouth, which were not there before. Second, it is probably not possible to interrupt the cognitive process without interfering with it and distorting it. The very process of questioning a person about his thought processes makes him self-conscious about them, brings to the fore values concerning rationality and orderliness, and perhaps even changes the content of his cognition toward considerations that are more easily verbalizable.

Until someone discovers a way to tap the cognitive process without interfering with it, we must rely mainly on observation of behavior during the process and on measurement of predicted end results of the hypothesized process. We may some day, perhaps, be clever enough to create circumstances under which observable behavior is a very direct indicator of the underlying cognitive process. For example, it might be possible to create an experiment in which, by observing the person's overt behavior, one can easily infer whether the person is reading a piece of information acceptingly and objectively or whether he is criticizing, deriding, and arguing against it.

At the moment we do not know how to create such an ingenious experimental situation. It is not difficult, however, to create one in which gross measures of information seeking and willingness to expose oneself to information can be obtained. It is easy for the experimenter to arrange sources of information so that he can observe what information a person chooses to read and how long he spends reading it. Thus, although one would not know in what manner, and with what attitude, a person was reading the information, one could measure the relative willingness to read one or another kind of material. One might expect such measurement to be rather gross since it reflects only one aspect of a process, but it should still be useful. In the pre-decision period one would expect to observe equal exposure to information favorable and unfavorable to all the alternatives. In the post-decision period one would expect to observe a preference for favorable information about the chosen alternative and for unfavorable material about the rejected alternative.

We know of no studies in the literature that have attempted

to compare pre-decision and post-decision information seeking in the same experimental situation. There are, however, several studies that have investigated selective information seeking in the post-decision period alone. An examination of these studies reveals that they do not provide any strong evidence to support our hypothesis about selectivity. Let us examine these studies briefly, since they throw some light on the methodological problems involved and also raise some questions concerning the validity of the hypothesis.

The typical study is one in which, during a period of time when post-decision dissonance may be presumed to exist, a measure is obtained of willingness to expose oneself to information that is clearly labeled as supporting or not supporting the choice. Thus, for example, Ehrlich *et al.* (1957), reasoning that post-decision dissonance would exist following the purchase of a new automobile, obtained measurements of the extent to which persons had noticed and read advertisements of automobiles subsequent to such a purchase. Advertisements about the car they had just purchased are, in a sense, clearly labeled as supporting their choice. Advertisements about the cars they considered but did not purchase are, in a similar sense, labeled as containing information not supporting their choice.

The results are equivocal. Those who have recently purchased a new car read more ads about that car than about other cars, but they do not avoid reading ads about the cars they considered but did not buy. They read just as many of these ads as ads about cars they never considered. Thus, there seems to be a preference for reading "own car" ads, but conceivably this preference may have existed before the decision. Perhaps that is why they chose to buy that car. Engel (1963), in reporting a study that obtains similar results, explicitly raises the question of the inadequacy of such non-experimental data as evidence for the existence of any selectivity of exposure to information in the post-decision period.

Another kind of study is exemplified by the experiments reported by Mills, Aronson, and Robinson (1959) and by Rosen (1961). In both these experiments subjects in college classes were offered a choice of one of two types of examination to take. Each student could choose to be examined by either an essay type or an objective type of examination. After choosing, they were told that they could have access to some articles concerning such examinations, and were asked to indicate which of a number of articles they would most like to read in preparation for the test. These articles were clearly identifiable by their titles as supporting either the choice of an essay examination or the choice of an objective examination. Thus, the subject's interest in reading each article could be used to measure the extent to which he preferred consonant or dissonant information.

The results of both of these studies are very similar. There is a small but significant preference for articles expounding positive aspects of the chosen alternative over articles expounding positive aspects of the rejected alternative. There is no indication of a preference for articles emphasizing negative aspects of the rejected alternative over articles stressing negative aspects of the chosen alternative. It is possible to interpret the results as indicating some preference for consonant over dissonant information. It is equally possible, and equally plausible, to interpret the data as simply indicating a preference for information that will be useful to the subjects. After all, the most useful kind of information would be that which explained how to do well on the type of examination the student had chosen. The authors of these experiments suggest that their results are due to the simultaneous operation of preference for consonant material and preference for useful material.

The most plausible conclusion one can reach from the existing data is that they suggest, but do not clearly demonstrate, that the presence of dissonance leads to selective exposure to information. If there is a selective process that favors consonant over dissonant information, the evidence in these studies may be obscured by the differential usefulness of information and the absence of any direct comparison between pre-decision and post-decision periods. It seemed worthwhile, then, to do an experiment in which one could obtain a direct comparison between the pre-decision period and the post-decision period. If one could arrange the content and context of the experiment so that all categories of information were equally useful to the subject, then, perhaps, the data would more clearly reveal selectivity of exposure to information in the post-decision period.

To accomplish this it would be desirable to have a situation in which a person had to choose between two alternatives, the choice having a marked effect on subsequent activity. In one condition the subject would be given an opportunity to look at information favorable and unfavorable to each alternative before making his choice. In another condition the same opportunity to look at the information would be given after the choice had been made. Such an experiment was conducted by Jecker and is reported below.

Experiment
Selective Exposure to New Information

Jon D. Jecker

One of the clear implications of the theory of cognitive dissonance concerns information-seeking activity. If dissonance exists, the person should seek out information that reduces dissonance and avoid information that increases dissonance. Hence, for example, the theory implies that after a person has made a decision, he should expose himself voluntarily to information that supports the choice he made and should avoid exposure to information that would indicate his choice was not good.

This implication of the theory of dissonance has not received adequate experimental support. Brehm and Cohen (1962), after careful review and analysis of the results of the relevant studies, come to the conclusion that these studies ". . . all failed to find evidence confirming the derivation that dissonant information will be avoided in proportion to the amount of dissonance produced. In each of these studies, while subjects sought out dissonance-*reducing* information, they did not necessarily *avoid* dissonance-*increasing* information." (P. 93.)

It is rather surprising that this implication of the theory has failed to be supported by experimental evidence when, at the same time, other closely related implications of the theory have received very adequate experimental support. Experimental evidence shows clearly that other manifestations of dissonance reduction do occur, and that the magnitude of the effects is related to the amount of dissonance created. It is with respect to the *information-seeking* aspect of the process of dissonance reduction that the data fail to support the theory. This, of course, is serious, since if we cannot obtain evidence to support the hypothesized process, major questions are raised about the validity of the entire interpretation.

One major inadequacy of all of the previous studies was the failure to control the usefulness of the various categories of information. If this variable were controlled, one might obtain results that would clarify the issue. In many situations information that is dissonance-increasing may actually be more useful to the person, and so, even though a tendency to avoid it exists, he may expose himself to it for reasons of its potential usefulness. Thus, for example, a person may have decided to take a certain trip by car rather than by a commercial airline. New information concerning road construction on his route, or snowy and icy conditions on the roads, would certainly increase dissonance for him after this decision. Nevertheless, in spite of a tendency to avoid this information, he might well expose himself to it, even seek it out, because such knowledge will be useful to him in coping with the consequences of his decision. It is useful to him to know whether he should take tire chains along, and it is useful to him to be able to estimate accurately how long he may be delayed en route by construction.

Consequently, we attempted to construct a decision situation of such a nature that dissonance-reducing and dissonance-increasing information would be equally useful to the person. The amount of exposure to these categories of information before and after the decision should provide data adequate to test the theory. The situation we used for the experiment was one in which the subject had to choose a partner to help him win a competitive game. We hoped that the four possible categories of information—positive and negative information about his partner's abilities, and positive and negative information about his opponent's abilities—would all seem of approximately the same usefulness for playing the game.

Three conditions were run in the experiment. In one condition subjects were given access to this information before being asked to choose which of two persons they wanted as their partner. Observation of what information they looked at, and for how long, would provide data concerning information seeking in the *pre-decision* period. In a second condition the subjects were given access to this same information *after* they had chosen their partners. This condition would, presumably, yield data concerning selectivity of information seeking in the *post-decision* period. In a third condition subjects were given access to the information after they had indicated whom they would prefer as their partner but while they were completely uncertain whether or not this preference would be taken into account in the actual assignment of partners for the game. Because of the evidence in the experiment reported by Jecker in Chapter 2 that under such circumstances dissonance-reduction processes do not begin, it was hoped that this condition would provide data concerning information-seeking behavior in a post-decision situation in which the person was *not attempting to reduce dissonance.*

Procedure

The subjects in the experiment were all male freshmen at Stanford University. They were contacted in English classes, where the experimenter asked them to volunteer to participate in an experiment that was described as being concerned with the relation between personality factors and strategy in competitive games. They were offered $2.00 each as payment for participation. Those who volunteered were later contacted by telephone and specific appointments were made.

When the subject arrived at the laboratory, he found two other students, actually confederates, taking part in the same session. The subjects had not been previously told that the experiment would require a group. The experimenter introduced himself and asked the subject and the two confederates to introduce themselves. Pretesting had indicated that conveying some information about the confederates to the subject was necessary in order to make the subject feel that he had some basis for making a choice. Consequently, the subject and the confederates were asked a few questions during the period of introduction. The confederates' responses to these questions were always the same, so that all subjects had the same information upon which they could form a first impression.

The experimenter repeated that he wanted to investigate the relationship between personality factors and the type of strategy chosen in a competitive game in a special situation where teams of unequal size were competing. The three "subjects" would be split into two sides, a two-man team versus an individual, and would then actually play a competitive game. The game was described as a complex war game involving strategy and tactics.

A commercial war game, "D-Day," was purchased, modified, and set up in the experimental room in full view. The experimenter described in some detail how the two sides would actually play. In pretests we had found that if the subject expected to be able to communicate actively with his partner, a differential was created in the perceived utility of information about the partner and about the opponent. Hence, in describing the game, the experimenter specifically stated that the members of the two-man team would not be allowed to communicate during the game itself. They would be on the same side, and both would win or lose as a team. They were to play, however, independently. As an added incentive, the experimenter stated that the winning team would receive a cash prize of $1.50 per person in addition to what they were being paid for participating in the experiment.

Before starting the game, the experimenter said he wanted to collect some information from each of the subjects by having them fill out a personality inventory. The inventory was described as a revision of a test that had been designed to measure the relationship between personality factors and problem-solving ability. The reliability and proven validity of the inventory made it very desirable and convenient for use in this experiment.

The experimenter then said that he would put the three "subjects" into separate rooms to fill out this personality inventory. The rationale for this was that he wanted to give each of them some different instructions and to have each of them do some different things. Also, the inventory would be completed faster if there were no distractions. The real subject was then left in the experimental room with his inventory materials while the experimenter presumably took the confederates to other rooms. Actually, the confederates' duties were completed at this point, and they departed. Throughout the remainder of the procedure, however, the experimenter continued to imply in his behavior that the confederates were in other rooms nearby.

When the subject finished his personality inventory, the experimenter took it and explained that he was going to collect all three answer sheets and have them analyzed immediately by machine. After three minutes, the experimenter returned, remarked that he had put the other two "subjects" to work, and proceeded to give additional instructions which differed, depending on the experimental condition.

The three experimental conditions were intended to differ with respect to when, in the decision process, the subjects were given an opportunity to read certain information. The information they were to be given was the results of the analyses of the personality inventories for the "other two subjects." This information was prepared, and presented, in the following form. At the proper time the experimenter brought into the room, and gave the subject, two IBM punch cards. In addition to an assortment of holes punched in it, each card had printed on it the name of one of the confederates. Alongside the name were printed two separate five-digit numbers.

These two cards had presumably just been produced by the IBM computer and represented the analyses of the personality inventories of the "other two subjects." It was explained that each of the two five-digit numbers on each card identified a dominant pattern of problem-solving behavior characteristics of that person as analyzed from his personality inventory. One of the numbers for each person identified a pattern of personality characteristics related to positive problem-solving abilities; the other number identified a pattern related to limitations the person had with respect to problem solving.

The subject was then shown a box containing many slides. He was told that in order to make the results of the machine analysis immediately and conveniently available to the subjects, detailed explanations of the meaning of all the possible personality patterns had been photographed on these slides. All that he had to do in order to understand the problem-solving behavior of each of the other two subjects was to take from the box those slides which bore the same numbers as appeared on the punch cards, put them into the slide projector on the table, and read them. To assist the subject, the experimenter put into another slide container all those slides from the original box that were relevant to the identified personality characteristics of the "two other sub-

jects." For each of the five-digit numbers that appeared on the
IBM cards there were three slides describing, and explaining, the
personality pattern. Thus, there were 12 relevant slides in all.
Three of them were clearly identified as containing favorable information about one of the "other subjects," three of them as
containing unfavorable information about that subject, and the
remaining two sets of three slides as containing favorable and
unfavorable information about the other one.

Each confederate was described by the slides in qualitatively
different terms but both were made to appear about equally desirable as partners in the competitive game. The slides described one
confederate as successfully intuitive in problem solving, very capable in handling information and making decisions, and very
adept at understanding a co-worker's approach to a problem. This
confederate, however, was unmotivated to work on a problem, easily distracted following a failure, and highly persuasible and in-
secure. The other confederate was described as successfully logical
and objective in problem solving, competent and economical at
procuring information, and very systematic in assessing alternative solutions. This confederate, however, reacted to failure by
concentrating excessively on the cause of the failure and by losing
sight of over-all success. He also exhibited an uncooperative, over-
confident attitude.

In all conditions the subjects were shown how to use the slide
projector and were told that they could read any or all of the 12
relevant slides. It was explained, however, that the amount of
time available was such that they would not be able to read all of
them carefully and thoroughly. In all conditions, it was emphasized that which slides he looked at, and how much of each he read,
was entirely up to the subject. While the subject was looking at
the slides, the experimenter kept a record of what specific slide
was being read, the order in which the subject read them, and how
much time he spent on each of the slides. If the subject had not
voluntarily stopped reading the slides at the end of ten minutes,
he was stopped by the experimenter.

The three experimental conditions differed as follows:

The Pre-Decision Condition. A short while after the subject had
completed his personality inventory, the experimenter returned
and showed him the two prepared cards and explained all about

the slides and their use. The experimenter then informed the subject that, on a random basis, he had been assigned to be on the two-man team to play the game against a single opponent. He was to choose whichever of the "other two subjects" he wanted as his partner on the team. The one he did not choose would be the team's opponent. The subject was told that he could use the information provided by the slides to help him choose his partner. If the subject did not indicate his choice before ten minutes had been spent looking at the slides, the experimenter stopped him and asked him to make his decision. Thus, in this condition, the subjects were given an opportunity to read the information before any decision had been made.

The Post-Decision Condition. In this experimental condition, parts of the procedure outlined above were reversed. The subject was similarly informed that he had been randomly assigned to be on the two-man team and that he was to choose his partner. He had to make his choice, however, on the basis of whatever impressions he had gained from the brief session when the subjects met and were introduced to each other. After the subject had chosen his partner, the experimenter brought him the same IBM cards and he was given the same opportunity to read the slides. The rationale for giving the subject access to the information, however, had to be different. In the pre-decision condition the subject was, of course, told that the information could help him make his decision. In the post-decision condition this reason was not applicable —the subject had already decided. The subjects in this condition were told, consequently, that the information on the good and bad aspects of the problem-solving behavior of both their partner and their opponent could be useful to them in actually playing the game. Hence, the subject was being given the opportunity to familiarize himself with any of the information that he cared to look at.

The Uncertain Condition. The subjects in this condition were treated like those in the post-decision condition in all respects except one. Each subject who was assigned to the uncertain condition was told that each of the three subjects would be asked to choose a partner and that the actual composition of the two-man team would depend on mutual choice. If two of them chose each other, they would constitute the two-man team and play against the third subject. If no mutual choices occurred, the experimenter would assign two of them to the team at random. Thus, in this condition the subject indicated a preference for a partner but did not know whether he would actually play with that partner. He might end up playing against the other two or he might be assigned to play in a team with the one he did not choose. This uncertainty about the actual composition of the team continued throughout the experiment. Thus, these subjects were exposed to the information after they had made a decision but while they were completely uncertain whether or not the decision would affect anything.

Shortly after each subject had read whatever slides he cared to read and had made his choice (or vice versa) he was asked to answer a questionnaire. This questionnaire asked him to write down each item of information that he had read about the other two subjects and to rate the importance of each of these items in the context of the game to be played. In all conditions the questionnaire was administered three minutes after the subject had finished reading the slides. When the questionnaire was completed, the experimenter went over it with the subject to be sure he understood the subject's interpretation of each of the items he had written down. The experiment was then over. The subjects did not actually ever play the game. The experimenter, of course, explained the true purpose of the experiment and the deceptions that had been used, and discussed the experiment with the subject at length.

Eighty-three subjects were used in the process of setting up and running the experiment. Twenty-two of these subjects were used in preliminary runs and pretesting. Changes were then made in the procedure to make the personality descriptions of the confederates more nearly equal in attractiveness and to provide more reality to the description of the game they were to play. Sixty-one subjects were run in the final experiment. The data from two subjects who misunderstood the instructions were discarded from the analysis. This left 20 subjects in the pre-decision condition, 20 in the post-decision condition, and 19 in the uncertain condition.

Four undergraduates served as confederates in the experiment, two of them at any one time, of course. Owing to problems of scheduling, no attempt was made to control the pairing of confederates among conditions.

Results

The amount of time subjects spent reading information supporting or not supporting the decision they had made, or were about
to make, should reflect any selective information seeking that may
exist. In order to be able to interpret these data reasonably, however, it is important to know whether or not the information provided about the "other two" was reasonably equated. That is, the
attempt to make the two confederates seem equally attractive as
partners may not have been successful. If the descriptions pictured
one confederate as better than the other, this could result in a
greater tendency to choose him and, perhaps, in a greater amount
of time spent on material favoring him simply because the material
was more important and more interesting. An examination of the
choices made in the pre-decision condition, however, provides
reassuring evidence. Since in this condition the subjects made their
choices after having read the information, any imbalance in the
descriptions would result in one confederate's being chosen more
often than the other. Actually, the choices split very evenly—11
subjects chose the confederate associated with one of the descriptions and nine subjects chose the other one. Apparently the two
descriptions were roughly equated.

One other possible methodological problem exists. In two of
the conditions the subjects had to choose their partners before seeing information about either confederate, and hence this choice
had to be based solely on first impression. If first-impression preferences for one or another confederate existed, this could affect
the results. This possibility can be examined in the post-decision
and uncertain conditions by computing, for each confederate, the
number of times he was chosen as a partner divided by the number
of times he participated as a confederate. One finds that there is,
indeed, a problem. The most popular confederate was chosen 78
per cent of the time. The other three were roughly equal, being
chosen 42 per cent, 38 per cent, and 33 per cent of the times they
appeared. The results, consequently, were inspected separately for
those subjects who chose the most popular confederate. On all the
measures that were computed, the results for these subjects are
strikingly similar to the results for the others. As far as can be
judged, the methodological problem is not serious.

TABLE 4.1

Time (in Seconds) Spent Reading Information

| | Experimental Condition | | |
	Pre-Decision	Post-Decision	Uncertain
Supporting Information	154.1	211.4	192.3
Non-supporting Information	152.4	189.0	184.9
Difference Divided by Total*	.00	+.04	+.02

* Computed for each subject separately and then averaged. A plus sign indicates a preference for supporting information.

Exposure to Information. Table 4.1 presents the data on the amount of time spent reading supporting and non-supporting information. Favorable information about the chosen (or to-be-chosen) confederate and unfavorable information about the rejected (or to-be-rejected) confederate is regarded as supporting information. The other two types are, of course, non-supporting.

The results in Table 4.1 do not reveal any post-decision selectivity in exposure to information. The subjects in the post-decision and in the uncertain conditions spend more time reading supporting information than do subjects in the pre-decision condition, but they also spend more time reading non-supporting information. The most plausible summary of these results is that the subjects in the pre-decision condition simply spend less total time reading the slides than do subjects in the other two conditions. An analysis of variance on the total time yields a significant F of 5.37 (beyond the 1 per cent level). Perhaps this indicates an increased interest in any relevant information in the post-decision period. Such an interpretation is supported by a study by Adams (1961), who reports that subjects experiencing dissonance show a greater over-all interest in new information. One cannot, however, put great weight in this result, since it may be due to a simple difference in instructions. In the pre-decision condition the subjects were told to read whatever information they wanted to in order to make a choice. Thus, they may have felt some pressure to stop reading information as soon as they had decided which one to choose. In the other two conditions there was no such defined stopping point. This difference in the instructions could well have produced the obtained effect on total time spent reading the slides.

In order to draw a conclusion about selectivity of exposure to the information, one must examine the degree to which supporting information is preferred to non-supporting information. The last row in Table 4.1 presents an index reflecting this preference. For each subject the amount of time spent reading non-supporting information was subtracted from the time spent reading supporting information and divided by the total time that subject spent reading the slides. The average of this measure shows that there is no preference for one or another kind of information in the pre-decision condition. In the other two conditions there is some tendency to prefer supporting information. These tendencies are slight, however. An analysis of variance does not approach an acceptable level of significance. We must conclude that Table 4.1 offers no support at all for the hypothesis concerning selectivity of exposure to information.

Closer inspection of the data, however, led to the feeling that Table 4.1 does not tell the whole story. It seemed clear from looking at the sequential pattern of slide viewing that behavior in the earlier portions of the sequence was somewhat different from behavior in the later portions. Actually, in all the experimental conditions there was a high degree of uniformity with respect to one aspect of slide viewing. Most of the subjects read at least one slide from each of the four patterns, and after having thus "scanned" the entire set of available information, went back to read additional material. Of the 59 subjects in the experiment, 48 did this. Only 11 subjects ever returned to read a slide from a previously sampled pattern before having scanned all four patterns. Hence it is convenient to examine viewing behavior during this period when the subjects were scanning the entire set of available information.

To do this we computed the time spent on supporting and non-supporting information during the scanning period, that is, before the subject repeated a pattern he had already sampled. For the 11 subjects who did not show this precise sequence of behavior, the cutting point for this analysis was the point at which they had sampled at least one slide from each pattern. Repetitions that oc-

TABLE 4.2

Time (in Seconds) Spent Reading Information During
"Scanning" Period

| | Experimental Condition | | |
	Pre-Decision	Post-Decision	Uncertain
Supporting Information	133.2	172.3	156.9
Non-supporting Information	126.9	140.2	151.1
Difference Divided by Total*	+.02	+.10	+.01

* Computed for each subject separately and then averaged. A plus sign indicates a preference for supporting information.

curred before this point were retained in the analysis. Table 4.2 presents these data.

The data from this scanning period present a somewhat different picture from the data seen earlier. The figures in the last row of Table 4.2 show some appreciable differences among the conditions in preference for supporting information. In the post-decision condition there is, on the average, 10 per cent more time spent on supporting information than on non-supporting information. The preference for supporting information in this condition is significantly different from zero ($t = 2.09$) at the 5 per cent level. Subjects in the other two conditions show no preference for supporting information during the scanning period.

An analysis of variance on these data, however, yields an F of only 2.04, not an acceptable level of significance. This result is due primarily to high variability in the pre-decision and in the uncertain conditions. This becomes clear if we simply look at the number of subjects in each condition who showed a preference for supporting information during the scanning period. In the pre-decision condition, 11 of the 20 subjects show such a preference; in the uncertain condition, 9 out of the 19 subjects show this preference; in the post-decision condition, however, 17 out of the 20 subjects spend more time reading supporting than non-supporting information. Chi-square computed for these data, yields a value of 6.68, which, for 2 degrees of freedom, is significant at the 5 per cent level.

There is, thus, some suggestion of selectivity in exposure to information in the post-decision condition. There is no evidence of any selectivity of exposure in either the pre-decision or the uncertain condition. In other words, during the period of conflict, when a person is making his decision, there seem to be no biasing tendencies in what information he wants to obtain. This is, of course, consistent with the results presented in Chapter 2, in which we found no evidence of any systematic re-evaluation of the alternatives in the pre-decision period. Similarly consistent with the evidence from the Jecker experiment reported in Chapter 2 is the result for the uncertain condition. Only after the person has made a clear-cut decision with definite consequences do we observe any evidence at all of selective exposure to information.

Dissonance Reduction. If one is to interpret the data as indicating that selective exposure to information occurs only in the service of dissonance reduction, it is important to demonstrate some link between this selectivity and subsequent dissonance reduction. The measurements of recall of the information that were obtained at the end of the experimental session give us an opportunity to see whether or not such a link exists.

To the extent that dissonance reduction would be indicated by differential recall of information, one would expect that in the post-decision condition, in which we saw evidence of selective exposure, we would also observe selective recall. That is, subjects in the post-decision condition might be expected to recall more information supporting their decision than information not supporting it. If for the pre-decision condition the recall measure had been obtained before subjects made their decisions, one would expect that, just as they showed no evidence of selective exposure, they would show no evidence of selective recall. However, the recall measure was obtained at the end of the experiment, after the subjects in this condition *had* made their decisions. Hence, with respect to the measure of recall, it is not a "pre-decision" condition. Dissonance reduction would have occurred after the decision and one may well expect to observe selective recall as evidence of this dissonance reduction.

How, then, can we examine the relation between selective exposure and selective recall? Fortunately, the uncertain condition allows us to make a relevant comparison. To the very end of the experiment the subjects in this condition remained uncertain who their partner, if they had one, would be. Under these conditions of uncertainty, there was no selective exposure to information. If the absence of selective exposure indicates an absence of any dissonance-reduction process, then one should not expect any selectivity in recall of information in the uncertain condition. Table 4.3 presents the relevant data on recall of supporting and non-supporting information for the three experimental conditions. In this table quotation marks are put around the label of the pre-decision condition to remind the reader that, on the recall measure, it is a post-decision condition in reality.

A glance at Table 4.3 reveals that there are no material differences among the conditions in the number of supporting items recalled. An analysis of variance here yields an F of less than 1.0. There are, however, striking differences in the number of non-supporting items recalled. The subjects in the uncertain condition recall more such items than do subjects in the other two conditions. An analysis of variance on these numbers yields an F of 5.96, which is significant beyond the 1 per cent level. It is clear that in the uncertain condition there is no selectivity of recall just as there was no evidence of selectivity in exposure. In the post-decision condition and in the "pre-decision" condition there is evidence of dissonance reduction reflected in excess recall of supporting information. One can also compute for each subject the number of supporting items minus the number of non-supporting items, divided by the total number of items recalled. The obtained mean indices for the three conditions are: "pre-decision" $= +.29$, post-decision $= +.21$, uncertain $= +.01$. An analysis of variance of

TABLE 4.3

Mean Number of Items of Information Recalled

Type of Information	Experimental Condition		
	"Pre-Decision"	Post-Decision	Uncertain
Supporting the Decision	3.40	3.35	3.05
Not Supporting the Decision	1.80	2.30	3.05

NOTE: Each item recalled was categorized as "supporting" or "not supporting" on the basis of the subject's interpretation of that item, not on the basis of which pattern actually contained the particular item.

these indices yields an F of 3.54, significant at the 5 per cent level. The mean for the uncertain condition is significantly different from either of the other two means. It seems clear that there is, indeed, a link between selective exposure and selective recall. Both seem to operate in the service of dissonance reduction and not otherwise.

The similarity in the recall data for the post-decision and "pre-decision" groups is rather striking. One might have expected a difference between these two conditions, since the "pre-decision" subjects were not selective at all in their exposure to the information and, presumably, were not paying selective attention to different categories of information. Whatever dissonance reduction occured in this condition must have occurred after they had *finished* looking at all the information and had made their decisions. Subjects in the post-decision condition, on the other hand, were presumably reducing dissonance while they were looking at the information. It is, hence, a bit surprising to see as much, or more, selective recall in the "pre-decision" as in the post-decision condition.

Examining the data a bit more closely, however, we do find differences between these two conditions. If the subjects in the post-decision condition were, indeed, paying selective attention to different categories of information and trying to reduce dissonance while reading the information, one might expect that this would be reflected in more reinterpretation of the information that they had read. That is, one might expect to find that in the post-decision condition subjects had succeeded in interpreting information that was bad about the chosen partner as really being good about him, and interpreting information that was good about the person he did not choose as actually being bad. In order to examine this, each item that was recalled was scored for dissonance-reducing reinterpretations (interpreting an item from a non-supporting pattern of information as being supporting) and dissonance-increasing reinterpretations (interpreting an item from one of the supporting patterns as being non-supporting). Each subject was then given a net score calculated by subtracting the number of dissonance-increasing interpretations from the number of dissonance-reducing interpretations.

The average net reinterpretation scores are +.25 for the "pre-decision" condition, $+.70$ for the post-decision condition, and $-.05$ for the uncertain condition. An analysis of variance yields an F of 4.25, significant at almost the 2 per cent level. The mean for the post-decision condition is the only one that is significantly greater than zero $(t = 3.85)$. It is also significantly greater than the mean for the uncertain condition $(t = 2.88)$. The difference between the means of the post-decision and "pre-decision" conditions yields a t of 1.75, significant between the 5 per cent and 10 per cent levels. In short, there is evidence that subjects in the post-decision condition, reducing dissonance while reading the information, tended to reinterpret items in a dissonance-reducing manner. In the "pre-decision" condition, since they were not reducing dissonance while reading the information, they do not use this mode of dissonance reduction as much. In the uncertain condition, in which no dissonance reduction at all occurred, there is clearly no reinterpretation in any selective manner. The data support the notion of a close link between selective exposure to information and the process of dissonance reduction.

Summary

Three experimental conditions were run to examine the question of selective exposure to information. In one condition subjects were given an opportunity to examine information before making a decision; in another condition the same opportunity was provided after the subject had made a definite, binding decision; in a third condition the opportunity to look at the information was provided after a decision that had uncertain consequences was made.

The data point to the conclusion that selective exposure occurs only when a dissonance-reduction process is going on. In the pre-decision period no such selectivity seems to occur. Likewise, no selectivity occurs in a post-decision period in which, because of uncertainty of outcome, no dissonance reduction takes place. Only in the post-decision period following a definite decision is there any evidence at all for selectivity in exposure to new information.

The evidence for the occurrence of selective exposure is, however, quite weak—just as it has been in all previous studies. To the extent that it occurred in our study, it occurred only during the initial part of the information exposure process. Weak though the evidence is, we may be justified in placing reliance on it because the data also show a clear and close link between this selectivity and the general dissonance-reduction process.

∎

At the beginning of this chapter we made the point that previous studies that had investigated selectivity of exposure to new information after the arousal of dissonance had uniformly found very weak results. The experiment reported by Jecker on the preceding pages represents an attempt to improve procedurally on previous studies. There is better control, in the Jecker study, over the factors entering the decision, the usefulness of the various categories of information, and there is, certainly, relatively good measurement of the amount of voluntary exposure to the new information. And yet, the evidence for post-decision selective exposure to information is as weak as that found by any of the previous studies.

Let us be clear about the nature of the evidence. The slight indication of selective exposure to information in the post-decision period comes only from the data on the initial scanning time, and not at all from the total exposure time. As a matter of fact, if we compare Table 4.1 with Table 4.2, it becomes clear that after the scanning period there is some tendency for subjects in the post-decision condition to prefer to read *non-supporting* information. After the scanning period, subjects in the post-decision condition read additional supporting material for about 39 seconds, on the average, as compared to about 49 seconds spent reading non-supporting slides.

How can we reconcile these data with the hypothesis that in the post-decision period there is a tendency to seek supporting, and to avoid non-supporting, information in order to reduce the existing dissonance? Worrying about this problem led us to the realization that all the studies that have been oriented toward the investigation of avoidance of dissonant information have been trapped by a peculiar problem. Consider the normal procedure

that such a study follows. After the creation of a state of dissonance, the subject is given an opportunity to read, or to indicate
a desire to read, any of a number of identified sets of material. In
order to obtain a measure of the extent to which the person prefers one type of material over another, the reading material is
always clearly labeled so that its dissonance-reducing or dissonance-increasing qualities are clear and unambiguous.

For example, in the Jecker study that has just been presented,
after the person has made a decision, he is told clearly that there
exists specific information that supports his decision and, also,
specific information that goes counter to the decision he made.
It seems clear that once the person has been told that the information exists that does not support his decision, additional dissonance has already been introduced—in a sense it is impossible for
him to avoid it since he knows it exists. These studies are not, then,
examining the question of avoidance of dissonance-increasing information. They are really investigating how a person deals with
increased dissonance that already has been introduced but is rather
contentless. That is, the person has the knowledge that there are
facts, or arguments, which do not support the decision he made,
but he does not know what these facts or arguments are.

How can the person cope with, and reduce, this additional dissonance? There might well be some tendency to avoid discovering
the concrete details of the information that is dissonant with the
decision, but without knowing the concrete details, it is very difficult to counterargue, reinterpret, and reduce the dissonance. It
is plausible to imagine, then, that if the person has some confidence
in his ability to deal effectively with the concrete aspects of the
new information, he will overcome his reluctance to read it and
will expose himself to these details with a critical attitude in
order to reduce the dissonance by counterarguing. The situation
is, perhaps, very similar to that encountered by a heavy cigarette
smoker who for many years has been more or less effectively dealing with the knowledge that cigarette smoking is harmful to his
health. When he notices a headline in the newspaper of another
speech or another study concerning the dangers of cigarette smoking, his initial tendency may be to ignore it. Usually, however,
he finally reads it very carefully and comes to the conclusion that
"it's just the same old stuff." In short, it may be very difficult to

reduce dissonance without coming to grips with the specific details of the information that creates the dissonance.

If this analysis of the problem is correct, it may indeed account for the weak results that experiments in this area have produced. It also makes the results of the preceding experiment by Jecker seem plausible. On the initial scanning of the information, there is a tendency to spend less time on material that is dissonant with the decision the person has made. But then the person goes back to the dissonant information in order to reinterpret it. And the evidence is that he succeeds in reducing dissonance to some extent by such reinterpretation.

This explanation of the persistent weakness of the results produced by experiments oriented toward the problem of selective exposure to new information may seem very much *ad hoc* and tenuous. It is certainly necessary to test this interpretation, and such a test is not difficult to devise. If a person is made to feel confident of his ability to reduce dissonance in a specific situation, we should find this person eager to expose himself to the dissonance-increasing information in order to come to grips with the details and reduce the dissonance. On the other hand, if a person is made to feel not at all confident of his ability to reduce dissonance in the situation, we would expect him to show a reluctance to encounter the specific details of the information. In the following pages Canon reports an experiment specifically designed to test these propositions.

Experiment
Self-Confidence and Selective Exposure to Information

Lance Kirkpatrick Canon

It seems plausible to maintain that people will avoid, whenever feasible, new information that is potentially dissonance-increasing. Previous studies, however, have tended to ignore the issue of when it is, and when it is not, feasible to avoid such information. In any given situation there may be many pressures unrelated to dissonance that could act to weaken such avoidance tendencies. In making predictions from the theory of dissonance, it is easy to forget all the other factors that, normally operating, can obscure the dissonance effect. Such things as general curiosity, desires to be well informed, and intellectual values about fairness and impartially are ubiquitous and would act in such a manner. In particular, there are two factors that would especially act to obscure the tendency to avoid dissonant information:

1. The Potential Usefulness of the Information. This variable has, indeed, been recognized as important by Mills, Aronson, and Robinson (1959), by Rosen (1961), and by Jecker in the experiment reported earlier in this chapter. The first two did not incorporate usefulness into their design, but recognized its possible confounding effects in their discussion. Jecker attempted, in a rough way, to make dissonant and consonant information equally useful. There is no way of assessing, however, the extent to which he succeeded.

The variable of "usefulness" of information is particularly important to examine, since it is possible that dissonance-arousing information may be, in some circumstances, intrinsically more useful. If a person is committed to a course of action, any information that can forewarn him of problems and difficulties is seen as much more useful than information that tells him how easy and pleasant it will all be. After all, these are the difficulties with which he will have to cope and these are the problems that he will have to solve. If this is true, then it is certainly important to incorporate the variable of usefulness into the design of any experiment on selective exposure to information, so that the precise effects of usefulness can be assessed.

2. Self-confidence about Dealing with Dissonant Information. This variable has not been recognized or discussed by previous investigators. Yet it is probably of major importance in determining the extent to which one may actually observe avoidance of dissonant information. Consider, for example, the studies by Mills, Aronson, and Robinson (1959) and by Rosen (1961). Dissonance was produced in these studies by giving college students a choice of whether they would take an essay examination or an objective examination in a course. College students have all, undoubtedly, had considerable experience with both kinds of examinations, know pretty well how they do on the different kinds, and know their own study habits, peculiarities, and abilities. A student who has chosen to take the essay examination and who is informed that there exist some articles on the disadvantages of essay examinations and on the advantages of objective examinations is probably quite confident of his ability to deal with such information. Even if some of the arguments in the articles are valid, they may be valid for others but not for himself. After all, he knows himself quite well. It is not surprising, then, that such a student would voluntarily read these articles and counterargue and reinterpret in order to reduce the dissonance aroused by the knowledge that these articles exist.

Feather (1963a, 1963b), for example, reports two studies in which he finds that subjects expose themselves equally to both dissonant and consonant information but are more critical in their approach to the dissonant material. Avoiding the dissonant information makes dissonance reduction rather difficult, since the person is then unacquainted with the details and does not know what to argue against. Only if he has little confidence in being able to deal with the new information would one expect to see marked evidence of avoiding the dissonant material. If our analysis is correct, it seems important to include self-confidence as a variable in the design of an experiment on selective exposure.

It seems reasonable to suppose that if a person is confident, and if dissonant material is seen as useful, one should observe a preference for reading the dissonant material. If, on the other hand, the dissonant material is not particularly useful, and if the person does not have much self-confidence, one would expect a very marked preference for consonant material. In order to assess the validity of these ideas, an experiment was conducted that manipulated both the perceived usefulness of dissonant information and the subject's self-confidence relevant to a decision.

Procedure

Eighty male subjects, 20 in each of four experimental conditions, were used in the experiment. They were all recruited from fraternities at San Jose State College. They were told that the study would take about one hour and that each fraternity would receive one dollar for each member who participated. Subjects were scheduled in groups of from four to seven but it was emphasized to them that they were each to work independently. There was no communication among the subjects until the experimental session was over.

The experimenter introduced himself as a representative of the "Bureau of Business Education Research" and described in considerable detail the history and goals of this fictitious organization. Ostensibly, the purpose of the study was to add data to a larger research program designed to lay the groundwork for the introduction of courses in "business and business policy" at the undergraduate level. The subjects were shown data indicating that no such courses were available at a large percentage of the colleges throughout the country and that polls on these campuses had shown considerable interest in such course work.

The subjects were told that the "Bureau" was attempting to standardize the best methods of presentation of this course material and to develop the most efficient instructional techniques. One method of presentation, the one with which they would actually be dealing, involved the analysis by the student of case studies taken from actual business problems. They were to be given a series of four such case studies, each of which would present a different situation and a different problem. The subject's task would be to read the case carefully, analyze the problem presented, and on the basis of this analysis choose between two alternative recommendations of the best possible solution to the problem.

It was further explained that, since the aim of the "Bureau" was to develop a course that would be of general interest and would be appropriate for persons with no business background, the cases had been selected and written in such a way that no special business aptitude or specific knowledge of business procedures was necessary for the successful completion of the case problems. It was stated, however, that a general ability to process and assimilate new information and to make decisions on the basis of such information was required, and that this ability was closely linked to general intelligence. Hence performance in the study should correlate fairly highly with general intelligence as measured by any of the standard IQ tests.

Finally, the effect of knowledge of results on learning was described as another of the goals of the study. The sometimes beneficial, sometimes deleterious, consequences of knowledge of results were discussed. All groups were told that they had been randomly selected as a group that would receive information telling them how well they had done after they had completed each case. Supposedly, other groups in the total study would not receive such treatment, and thus the effectiveness of these two teaching techniques could be compared.

Each subject was then handed a case-study booklet and an answer booklet. They were instructed to read the first case, think about it, and then indicate in the answer booklet which of the two alternative solutions they chose. The subjects were asked to signal when they had recorded their answers. When a subject signaled, the experimenter went over to his desk and made a note in his own records of the subject's answer. After all the subjects had finished the first case, the experimenter gave each of them a slip of paper bearing a statement of the following form: "Your answer to case number ——— was (correct, incorrect) as judged by the business experts who developed this case. ——— other persons in your group gave the same answer you did." The subjects were then allowed to turn to case 2 in the booklet. The same procedure was followed for the first three cases.

After completing the fourth case, the subjects were not given the usual feedback slip but instead were told that they would be asked to do something "a little different" with their analyses of this last case. Since the "Bureau" was also interested in gaining information about how people deal with such case problems, the subjects were now asked to participate in a written portion of the study. Each of them would take part either in a written "debate" or in developing a written "presentation of his point of view" concerning only the fourth case study. Stress was put on the fact that the experimenter did not care about compositional style, grammatical correctness, or any of the other formal properties of an essay.

It was explained that, since this was a somewhat more difficult task than simply making a decision as to the best alternative solution, a series of five articles had been prepared for the subjects' use in this written portion of the study. The authorship of these articles was ascribed to "graduate students who have worked with this case and other students like yourselves who have previously participated in the study." Since the subjects would not have time to read all the articles, and, further, since most persons would not want to see them all, the experimenter distributed a form that gave descriptive titles of the articles and asked each subject both to rate and to rank them in terms of the degree to which he wanted to have an opportunity to read each one. On the basis of this information the experimenter would try to see that each subject received his first two or three choices, which he could then examine for a period of time prior to working on the written essay. The importance of carefully rating and ranking *all* five articles, and not just singling out the first two or three choices from the remainder, was pointed out, "since there were only a limited number of certain articles" and thus it might not be possible to provide the first choices to everyone.

After the rating and ranking of the articles, and while the experimenter presumably was getting the preferred articles in order, the subjects completed a short questionnaire which called for ratings, on scales from 0 to 100, of (a) subjective confidence in the correctness of the decision made in the last case; (b) degree of difficulty experienced in coming to a decision on the cases in general; (c) extent to which participating in the study was an interesting experience; (d) extent to which the study has added to an understanding of the problem with which it was designed to cope; (e) degree to which special ability was required for successful performance on the case problems; and (f) degree to which the articles selected would be of assistance in work on the written discussion.

When all the subjects had completed this form, the experiment was called to a halt, the deception and the necessity for it were explained, and the subjects were asked not to discuss the nature of the study with those who had not yet participated. Informal checks indicated that this request was complied with.

During the course of this procedure, two experimental variables were manipulated to produce four different experimental conditions. In order to vary the perceived usefulness of contra-decisional information, different instructions were given concerning what the subject was asked to write following the decision he made on case 4. Those subjects who were randomly assigned to the "highly useful" condition were informed that they were to participate in a written debate concerning their decision on the fourth case. They would be provided with a mimeographed form on which there would be a number of probing questions posed from the point of view of a person supporting the alternative the subject had not chosen. Their task would be to combat these arguments represented by the written questions just as they might do in an oral debate. The reasoning behind this manipulation of usefulness was that, since the subject would have to respond to issues raised against his position, it would be more useful to him to have prior access to contra-decisional information so that he could plan his rebuttal.

The other half of the subjects were assigned to the "less useful" condition. These subjects were told that they were to write a presentation of their point of view concerning the fourth case and explain why they had chosen their solution. Thus, their task was to develop a forceful presentation of their own case. Not needing to rebut opposing arguments, these subjects should see less usefulness in having prior access to contra-decisional information.

Half of the subjects in each of the "usefulness" conditions were randomly assigned to the "high-confidence" condition. The intention was to indirectly manipulate the confidence the subject would have in being able to cope adequately with, and argue away, contra-decisional information. This was done by manipulating the "knowledge of results" they were given about their performance on the first three cases. The idea was that if they felt they frequently did poorly on this kind of task they would be more likely to anticipate difficulty in dealing with contra-decisional information than if they felt they usually did well. To create high confidence the feedback slip after each decision informed the subject that he had chosen the correct alternative on each case and that, each time, the majority of the others in the group had not been correct. To create low confidence the subjects were informed that they and the majority of others in the group had been correct on the first case. On the second and third cases the feedback slips informed them that they had chosen the *incorrect* alternative while the majority of others in the group had been correct.

It should be emphasized that the essay they were to write concerned only the fourth decision and that the subjects were not told anything about the correctness or incorrectness of their decisions on the fourth case. The decision in case 4 concerned whether a company should maintain its present modes of product distribution (solution A) or should employ new retailing methods (solution B). The five articles that they were asked to rate and rank according to how much they wanted to read them were specifically concerned with this fourth case. The titles of two of these articles supported solution A, two others supported solution B, and one was neutral. One article supporting solution A and one supporting solution B were positively worded; the others were negatively worded. The gist of the titles is the following:

The potential benefit to the company resulting from solution B,

The difficulties that the company will encounter if it continues to depend solely on solution A,

The case for the continued utilization of solution A,

Solution B—an inappropriate alternative method of retailing the company's goods,

The evolution of the company as a major producer.

All subjects, of course, were asked to rate and rank the same list of articles. Whatever their decision had been, two of the titles promised support for that decision and two of them promised contra-decisional information.

Results

Before we proceed to examine the main results of the experiment, it is necessary to take a brief glance at some data that may indicate a methodological problem. It will be recalled that, after the subjects had indicated their interest in reading each of the articles, and while the experimenter was presumably getting these articles ready, the subjects were asked to answer a questionnaire. These questions were intended mainly to provide data about the success of the experimental manipulations. Unfortunately, perhaps because the scales were poorly defined, perhaps because the subjects were impatient to read the articles, they tended to answer these questions quickly and without making good use of the scale. For example, on the first question which asked about their confidence in the correctness of their decision on the fourth case, more than half the subjects, presumably using a continuous 100-point scale, marked exactly 75 or 100. This is quite typical of their answers to all these questions. It is, hence, not surprising that this questionnaire produced no significant differences among the experimental conditions. It is unfortunate, however, that there is no evidence to support the effectiveness of the manipulations.

In writing the fourth case, the attempt was made, of course, to have the two solutions seem about equally attractive. Also, in writing the titles to the articles, the attempt was made to have them be of equal intrinsic interest—at least those four articles that were supportive or non-supportive of the decision. Some problem arises because these attempts were not completely successful. For all subjects, in all conditions combined, the mean interest rating (on a scale ranging from 0, very little desire to see the article, to 100, very great desire to see the article) for articles favoring solution A was 73.1, whereas the mean rating for articles favoring solution B was only 58.2. Clearly, the articles favoring solution A must have sounded intrinsically more interesting.

Apart from the increase in variability in the data that would result from this disparity in intrinsic interest, it would not be any great problem if the proportion of subjects who chose solution A was approximately the same in each of the four experimental conditions. This is almost, but unfortunately not quite, true. In three of the four conditions the number of subjects choosing solution A is very similar—11, 12, and 13 out of the 20 subjects in each condition. However, in the high-confidence—less-useful condition only six of the 20 subjects chose solution A. In the light of this a correction that would eliminate the effect of the difference in intrinsic interest was used on the data. The interest ratings for each subject for those articles favoring solution A were expressed as deviations from 73.1, the mean interest expressed in those articles for all conditions combined. Similarly, the interest ratings for those articles favoring solution B were expressed as deviations from 58.2. Thus, if a subject's average rating of the two articles supporting solution A was 80, he was given a score of +6.9 (80 − 73.1); if his average rating of the two articles supporting solution B was 40, he was given a score of −18.2 (40 − 58.2). If this subject had actually chosen solution A on the fourth problem, his preference for consonant over dissonant material would be +25.1. If the subject had

TABLE 4.4

Average Preference for Consonant Over Dissonant Articles
(Corrected Ratings of Interest)

	High Confidence	Low Confidence
Highly Useful	−14.3	+5.9
Less Useful	+8.2	+29.6

chosen solution *B*, his preference for consonant over dissonant material would be −25.1. The data will be presented in this corrected fashion.

Interest in New Information. Table 4.4 presents the average preference for consonant over dissonant material for each of the experimental conditions. It is clear from a casual inspection of the data in Table 4.4 that both the confidence variable and the usefulness variable have marked effects on the interest in reading supportive or non-supportive information. As confidence decreases, subjects are less willing to expose themselves to dissonant material. As the usefulness of the dissonant information decreases, subjects are also less willing to expose themselves to it. An analysis of variance shows that both of these main effects are highly significant statistically. The effect of usefulness yields an F of 11.96 and the effect of confidence yields an F of 9.73, both significant well beyond the 1 per cent level.

Let us look at the data a bit more closely. Not all of the conditions show preference for reading consonant rather than dissonant material. When the dissonant material is potentially useful, and if the person is rather confident that he can cope with it adequately, there is actually a very large preference for exposing oneself to the details of the dissonant information. Subjects in this condition, on the average, rate the non-supportive articles 14 points higher on the interest scale than the supportive articles. On the other hand, when there is no particularly useful purpose to be served by reading the dissonant information, and if the subjects are not very confident of being able to cope with its details successfully, one discovers a huge preference for the supportive material, a preference amounting to almost 30 points on the scale of interest. Clearly, the potential usefulness of the dissonant material and how well the person feels he can cope with the details of the dissonance that has already been introduced are both important variables.

It will be recalled that in addition to our having the subjects rate each article, they were asked to rank them. These data were obtained so that we could have a comparison of preference for consonant and dissonant articles which was independent of any possible differences among conditions in absolute level of interest in reading the articles. It turns out, however, that the rankings provide us with no additional information. There were no differences among the four conditions in absolute level of interest in reading articles. The average ratings of interest in reading the four relevant articles ranged from 65.2 to 66.4, small differences indeed. Actually, the ratings and the rankings correlate highly (above +.7 in each condition) and it is, hence, not surprising that the rankings yield the same pattern of results as the ratings.

The results of the experiment, that is, the effects of the two independent variables, certainly seem to provide a basis for understanding the weak effects obtained in previous studies. Lack of control over the perceived usefulness of the dissonant information, and lack of control over the confidence the subject feels in being able to reduce the dissonance if he exposes himself to its concrete details, would produce very large variability in the pattern of selective exposure. The over-all preference for consonant material could be expected to show itself weakly, if at all.

The data on the level of interest in reading the neutral article must also be examined. This article was included to provide some additional data on the general comparability of the four experimental conditions. There is, of course, no reason for the various conditions to differ in the amount of interest in reading this neutral, and somewhat irrelevant, article on the history of the company. The level of interest in reading this article was rather uniformly low. The mean interest ratings for the various conditions range from 24.2 to 34.2; none of the differences approaches an acceptable level of statistical significance.

One can also look at the data concerning the neutral article from another point of view. If there were active avoidance of the dissonant articles in any of the experimental conditions, one might expect that the interest level for the dissonant material would be lower than that for the neutral article. This is clearly not the case. Either there is no active avoidance of dissonant material in any of the conditions or the neutral article sounds intrinsically uninteresting or irrelevant to the problem at hand.

Comparison with Previous Findings. It is of interest to see how the results of this experiment compare with the results of previous experiments if one ignores the two independent variables and simply looks at the preference for consonant over dissonant material for all conditions thrown together. For all 80 subjects the mean preference for consonant over dissonant material is $+7.4$, a rather small difference on the scale of interest. This result is not dissimilar to the results of other studies.

Previous studies by Mills, Aronson, and Robinson (1959) and by Rosen (1961) have found that the preference for consonant material is greater when the titles of the articles are stated positively, but is almost nonexistent if the titles are stated negatively. Since two of the four articles in this study were positively worded (implying positive support for a particular solution) and two were negatively worded (implying an attack on a particular solution), the data can be examined to see if the same finding holds. It turns out that the data do show the same thing. For the positively worded articles the preference for consonant over dissonant material is $+12.4$; the comparable value for the negatively worded articles is only $+2.4$. A *t* test yields a value of 1.77, significant at the 8 per cent level. Although of borderline significance, the fact that this study does replicate the findings of previous studies is comforting.

The most plausible interpretation of this difference between positively and negatively worded titles is that the material which promises to point out difficulties and problems associated with the chosen action is seen as being more useful. If this interpretation is the correct one, the effect of the two independent variables in this experiment should not be changed by the positive or negative wording. Only the absolute level should be different. Table 4.5 presents the data on preference of consonant over dissonant material for the two types of articles separately.

It can readily be seen that, in each experimental condition, the preference for consonant over dissonant material is greater for the positively than for the negatively worded articles. The effects of the variables of usefulness and confidence are, however, the same. Regardless of whether the article is described as supporting a position or as attacking a position, the preference for consonant material increases as confidence decreases and as the potential use-

TABLE 4.5

Average Preference for Consonant Over Dissonant Articles

	High Confidence		Low Confidence	
	Positively Worded	Negatively Worded	Positively Worded	Negatively Worded
Highly Useful	−7.0	−21.6	+11.3	+1.0
Less Useful	+11.6	+4.8	+33.9	+25.4

fulness of the dissonant material decreases. The entire pattern of the data is quite consistent with the interpretation that when the titles are negatively stated, the perceived potential usefulness of the dissonant material is increased.

Summary

An experiment was done that examined the effects of the usefulness of dissonant information, and of self-confidence, on selectivity of exposure to new information.

In general, subjects prefer to read articles that support their decision. The less useful dissonant articles are, the greater is this tendency; also, the less confidence the person has in being able to cope with the dissonant material, the greater is the preference for consonant material. Subjects who were highly confident, and perceived dissonant information as useful, actually showed a strong preference for reading dissonance-increasing information.

The data obtained are consistent with the results of previous studies and help explain the weak results previously obtained concerning post-decision selectivity in seeking information.

∎

If we consider the previous research that has been done on the problem of selective exposure to information together with the results of both the Jecker and the Canon experiments reported in this chapter, we may begin to have a better understanding of the process. It does seem plausible, in the light of the data, to assert that information seeking in the pre-decision period is not selective but is rather objective and impartial. No evidence exists to the contrary and, indeed, the Jecker experiment provides supporting evidence. Unless there is an active process of dissonance reduction going on, there is no evidence of selective exposure that favors potentially consonant over potentially dissonant material.

When dissonance does exist and when there is an active dissonance-reduction process occurring, then there does seem to be evidence for selective exposure to new information so as to help in the dissonance-reduction process. The above sentence, it should be noted, is a rather different statement from that made by Festinger (1957). In discussing this question he states: "If (a person) is led, for one reason or another, to expect (an information source) will produce cognitions which will increase consonance, he will expose himself to the information source. If the expectation is that the cognition acquired through this source would increase dissonance, he will avoid it." (P. 128.)

In the light of our current knowledge acquired from experimental work, we must come to the conclusion that this statement is oversimplified. It is obviously not correct to assert such simple avoidance of material that is seen as potentially dissonance-increasing. First, it seems clear that precisely this kind of material is frequently seen as useful and is, hence, sought out for reasons of its usefulness. Second, it seems clear also that under conditions in which the person feels confident, he will actively expose himself to this "dissonant" material in order to counterargue. Only under special circumstances, which we now understand more clearly as a result of the experiment by Canon, will one observe an active avoidance of potentially dissonant material.

Thus, it is undoubtedly more correct to say that selective exposure to new information will occur in the service of dissonance reduction. When the person perceives that dissonance will be effectively reduced by exposing himself to and coping with the details of the dissonant information, one will certainly not observe avoidance of it. Avoidance of potentially dissonance-increasing information would be useful in the service of dissonance reduction only if the person feels unable to cope with the new information in its details. And, of course, such avoidance would be observed only under circumstances where other reasons for exposure, such as usefulness or curiosity, were absent.

Chapter Five

The Post-Decision Process

■

We have now come to the point where we can examine the post-decision process in somewhat more detail. From our theory, and from much of the experimental evidence that we have presented, one is clearly led to the conclusion that the act of decision makes a crucial difference. The act of decision initiates a qualitative change in the cognitive process.

It seems important, then, to consider the immediate post-decision situation. Since we know that the process changes, it is of interest to know the exact nature of the transition from one to another process. Are the effects of the decision immediate? Is the transition sudden or gradual?

To help us start thinking about the matter, let us go back to our conclusions about the interaction between pre- and post-decision processes. On the basis of the experimental evidence presented in Chapters 2 and 3, we asserted that the greater the extent to which existing information is considered and thought through before dissonance exists, the more rapidly and effectively does dissonance reduction proceed after dissonance has been created. How might the transition from pre- to post-decision processes proceed in order to produce this kind of result?

If the pre-decision period is, indeed, spent mainly in impartially evaluating both the positive and the negative aspects of each alternative, then the more the person has done this, the more he knows about each alternative at the moment of making his decision. Furthermore, as we know from the previous chapters, after the usual type of decision is made the cognitive process of dissonance reduction begins. But, undoubtedly, it takes time and cognitive work in order to change one's evaluations effectively so as to reduce dissonance. If the cognitive work has already been done, the process of dissonance reduction may proceed quickly. If the various aspects of the alternatives were not very well thought through in the pre-decision period, this process of examination must take place in the post-decision period in order to facilitate the reduction of dissonance.

The foregoing account implies that in order to reduce dissonance in the post-decision period, the person is mainly preoccupied with attending to the dissonance that exists. Hence we are led to propose the following characteristic of the transition from pre-decision to post-decision process. As soon as the decision is made, all the negative aspects of the chosen alternative and all the positive aspects of the rejected alternative become salient for the person. In other words, immediately after the decision the person focuses his attention on the dissonance that exists and, of course, attempts to reduce it. This notion of immediate post-decision salience of dissonance has already been suggested by Brehm and Cohen (1962), who also present the results of an experiment to support the idea.

In that experiment each subject was asked to check, on a list, the personality characteristics that he possessed. He was also asked to check the same list about a close friend of his. Each subject was then shown an artificially prepared list supposedly checked about him by his close friend. On this artificially prepared list a certain number of items were checked by his friend exactly as he had checked them about himself. A certain number were checked differently, however. In other words, on a certain number of items he was evaluated differently by his friend from the way he saw himself. These items presumably introduced dissonance. Brehm and Cohen report that immediately after the subject had seen the artificially prepared check list, there was a preponderance of recall of the dissonance-producing items. After a period of a few days, however, consonant items were primarily remembered.

While such data lend some support to the idea of immediate post-decision salience of dissonance, the support is rather weak. For one thing, the data do not pertain to a post-decision situation. But this is perhaps a minor point. More important is the fact that the data are amenable to other, simpler interpretations. One could explain the immediate-memory result very readily in terms of contrasting items being easily noticed rather than in terms of salience of dissonance. One would, obviously, like to have better corroboration.

Let us consider some of the consequences to be expected if there does, indeed, exist such immediate post-decision salience of dissonance. Phenomenally, such salience of dissonance might be experienced as a feeling of regret, something that most of us have felt, probably, at one time or another. A person, for example, may shop around for an automobile to buy, investigate several kinds, and finally decide on which to purchase. As soon as the purchase is accomplished and final, he may very well be assailed by a sudden feeling of "Oh, my, what have I done!"

Others have noted this type of phenomenon. Lewin (1938), for example, says: ". . . frequently after the decision is made, the goal not chosen seems to be the more attractive one . . . ." (Pp. 206–7.) The existence of such post-decision regret was also noted by Festinger (1957) in his statement of the theory of cognitive dissonance. In this statement, however, Festinger probably misinterprets the phenomenon. He discusses it as perhaps a defensive reaction to avoid dissonance. He states: "Avoiding post-decision dissonance can also be accomplished to some extent by psychologically revoking the decision as soon as it is made. Thus, for example, if immediately after having made a decision, irrevocable though it may be in actuality, the person is convinced that it was absolutely the wrong thing to do, he is again preparing himself for the impact of possible dissonance and avoiding this impact." (P. 270.)

It seems much more likely that such post-decision regret is simply the manifestation of the fact that the dissonance has suddenly become salient. After all, if after the choice is made the person's attention becomes spontaneously directed mainly toward the bad aspects of the chosen alternative and the good aspects of the rejected alternative, it would seem reasonable for him to feel regret and to think that perhaps he did the wrong thing.

How can we test this interpretation adequately? After all, if such post-decision regret is due to sudden salience of dissonance, it must be a rather momentary affair in most experimental decision situations. There is certainly enough experimental evidence that very shortly after the decision one may observe an increase in

relative preference for the chosen alternative. Thus, at least for the
kinds of decisions we can deal with in the laboratory, it would
seem that any manifestations of post-decision regret would be
observable only momentarily. The very process of rerating the
alternatives after the decision may, in many cases, provide enough
time for dissonance reduction to overcome the regret.

One possible test procedure suggests itself, however. If, during
the period when dissonance is salient, a person were given the
opportunity to reconsider, he should show some inclination to
reverse his decision. Thus, if we could produce a situation in
which *immediately after* having made a decision the person is
asked to make the decision, we should obtain an excessive amount
of decision reversal. The preceding sentence may sound like gib-
berish, but it is possible to approximate such a condition plausibly.
Festinger and Walster report such an experiment below.

Experiment

Post-Decision Regret and Decision Reversal

Leon Festinger and Elaine Walster

The purpose of this experiment was to ascertain whether or not
there is a tendency to reverse one's decision immediately after
making it. If there is such a tendency, this would provide some
evidence for the hypothesis concerning the immediate post-decision salience of dissonance.

There is, of course, some difficulty in creating a laboratory situation in which it is plausible to ask a person to make a decision
twice, especially if one wants the second decision to occur with
minimum time delay after the first. The idea for how to set up
such an experimental situation was suggested to us by an experiment by Brehm, Cohen, and Sears (1960). In this experiment there
was an attempt to obtain both pre-decision and post-decision
ratings of the alternatives involved in a choice. This was done in
the following way. The subject was asked to rank each of a number

of objects. He was then told that he would have a choice between the objects he had ranked third and fourth as a free gift. The experimenter asked the subject not to make his decision yet, but first to rank all the objects again. After he had finished the reranking, the subject was asked to make his choice.

A rather striking, and somewhat baffling, methodological problem arose in this experiment. Of a total of 49 subjects, 20 chose the object that they had originally ranked fourth. In short, 40 per cent of the subjects chose the alternative that they had considered the less attractive. While it is possible that this could have occurred simply because of very low reliability of the initial ranking, this does not seem plausible. Forty per cent seems like a very high figure.

The theoretical idea about post-decision regret suggested another explanation. The subjects in this experiment knew, when they performed the second ranking, which two objects they would be asked to choose between. The process of making the second ranking under these circumstances virtually forced them to make a choice. Since they must rank one of the two objects higher than the other, and since they know they must choose between these two objects, this ranking is close to expressing a decision. Immediately after having expressed this "decision" they were asked to choose between the two objects. It is possible that salience of dissonance following the decision expressed by the ranking procedure could account for the very high rate of decision reversals when they were asked to state their choice formally.

The present experiment, designed to test the hypothesis concerning post-decision regret, was modeled along these same lines. Subjects would be asked to rank a number of objects before being asked to make a choice. During the process of ranking, subjects in one condition would know, whereas subjects in the other condition would *not* know, which two objects they would be asked to choose between. If our hypothesis is correct, the former group would, after the ranking, experience regret and would show a high proportion of decision reversals, that is, ultimate choice of the alternative originally rated as less attractive. The latter group, of course, not knowing anything about the choice alternatives while they made the ranking, would not be making a decision and, hence, could not experience post-decision salience of dissonance after the ranking. Hence, this group should not show as many decision reversals.

Procedure

Sixty-eight female students at Stanford University were used as subjects in the experiment. Forty-nine of these came from the course in introductory psychology, the other 19 from other courses. All subjects knew beforehand that they were to participate in some market research concerning hair styles.

Each subject was scheduled individually for the experiment. When the subjects arrived at the appointed time and place, they were led into a room through a door marked "Market Research—Duart-Clairol, Inc." The room contained several large posters advertising permanents and tints. Various hair style magazines were conspicuously displayed on a table.

Each girl was handed 12 photographs of different hair styles and told to examine them until she was familiar with all of them. After about two minutes and while the subject still had the photographs before her, she was asked to rate the attractiveness of each one. Specifically, the subject was told: "Considering your face and figure—and whatever else you would take into consideration—rate how you would feel about having your *own* hair done in each of these hair styles." The ratings were done on a 13-point rating scale on which 1 was described as "I would like to have my hair done in this style extremely much," 7 as "I don't know if I would like to have my hair done in this style or not," and 13 as "I would dislike having my hair done in this style extremely much."

When the subject had completed this initial rating of the 12 hair styles, she was given another task that consisted of choosing attractive trade names for various hair colors. The purpose of this second task was merely to fill some time with seemingly appropriate things. While the subject was thus engaged, the experimenter examined the ratings she had just completed in order to select two hair styles that the subject would later be asked to choose between. In order to have the choice be as similar as possible, psychologically, to all subjects, to avoid the use of alternatives that were actually disliked, and to prescribe a strict procedure for the experimenter, the following criteria were used in the selection of the two hair styles:

1. Both styles had to be appropriate for the subject's hair length.

2. The two styles had to be rated exactly one unit apart on the 13-point rating scale.

3. No style rated lower than 7, the neutral point, was to be used, nor was the style rated as the most desirable to be used.

4. Among the pairs of hair styles that met these qualifications, that pair was chosen which was rated more attractive. Thus, if possible, those hair styles rated second and third best were chosen.

It was not always possible to satisfy all these conditions completely. Under such circumstances, requirement 2 was sacrificed. Thus, seven subjects had alternatives separated by two units, and five subjects had alternatives separated by half a unit. These exceptions were divided as equally as possible between the two conditions.

After the experimenter had made the selection of the two hair styles that were to be used later for the choice and after the subject had completed the second task, she was asked to *rank* the 12 hair styles which she had previously rated. Rank 1 would indicate "Would most like to have my hair done in this style," while rank 12 would indicate "Would least like to have my hair done in this style." At this point the procedure for the two experimental conditions diverged.

"No-Prior-Decision" Condition. In this condition the subjects proceeded to rank the 12 pictures according to the instructions. After the ranking was completed, the experimenter said: "Now that you've finished the ranking, I can give you some information." The subject was then told that when Duart-Clairol asked to interview psychology students, the Department of Psychology was not very enthusiastic about it. They felt that students would learn very little by participating in such an "applied" study. Hence the Department felt that the company should somehow recompense the students for their time. The company agreed to offer each participant a free haircut and hair set at a nearby salon. However, the subject was told, since the company was interested in seeing the relation between preferences and hair characteristics, she could not have her hair set in just any style. She could have her hair done in "whichever of these two styles" she preferred.

At this point the experimenter handed to the subject the photographs of the two hair styles that had previously been selected. The subject was asked to indicate which one she wanted. When the subject made her choice, the experimenter wrote it down on a "free coupon" that was given to the subject to present at the salon.

"Prior-Decision" Condition. The only difference between the procedure for this condition and the one already described was the order of events. All instructions were otherwise identical. Just as the subject took the 12 photographs and was about to begin to rank them, the experimenter said, "Oh, I might as well tell you now," and then proceeded to give her "information" identical to that in the other condition. At the conclusion of the information statement, the experimenter put paper clips on the two photographs which the subject was to choose between, so that they were clearly identifiable to the subject, and said, "Don't tell me which one you want now. We'll talk about it later. Right now, just finish the ranking." The experimenter then looked away to discourage conversation.

As soon as the ranking was completed, the experimenter asked the subject to choose the one she wanted for her free hairdo and wrote the information on the free coupon as in the other condition.

Thus, in the prior-decision condition the subject knew that she was going to choose between two particular hair styles during the time that she was doing the ranking. In this condition, then, the rank order of those two hair styles is an expression of a decision by the subject. In the no-prior-decision condition, on the other hand, the subject did not even know she was to make a choice while doing the ranking. Thus, for this condition, the first time the subject made a decision was when she was asked to indicate her choice at the completion of the ranking.

In both conditions, after the subject had indicated her choice and had been given her free coupon, she was asked to evaluate the 12 hair styles once more on rating scales identical to those used for the initial rating. The excuse used for this second rating was that the "company thought it was possible that the girls' preferences might be influenced by the academic setting we're in." The experimenter then asked the girl to think about dorm friends and activities for a few seconds to "get into a dorm-like mood" and then to do the ratings.

After the completion of these final ratings, the experiment was over. The purpose of the experiment was fully explained to each girl.

Results

Our main interest in the data is to compare the initial ratings made by the subject with the hair style she finally chose. The reader will recall the theoretical expectations concerning this. Subjects in the prior-decision condition, at the time they are asked to state their choice, should be experiencing salience of post-decision dissonance, since, in essence, they have just expressed their decision in the ranking. Consequently, one would expect that there would be a higher incidence of decision reversal in this condition than in the no-prior-decision condition. A decision reversal would be an instance in which the subject, when asked finally which style she wanted, chose the hair style that she had initially rated as less attractive. In short, post-decision regret, if it existed, should lead to tendencies toward decision reversal.

The data are quite clear on this matter. In the no-prior-decision condition, out of a total of 36 subjects, ten (28 per cent) chose the less attractive alternative. In the prior-decision condition, out of a total of 32 subjects, 20 (62 per cent) chose this less attractive alternative. The difference is highly significant. Chi-square is equal to 8.33, significant beyond the 1 per cent level. In short, the prior-decision condition does indeed show a high incidence of decision reversal. We may take this as evidence that post-decision regret is, indeed, a general occurrence.

One can, of course, question why the percentage who choose the initially less attractive alternative is so high in the no-prior-decision condition. The figure of 28 per cent decision reversals might be due simply to the unreliability of the initial ratings, or it might be due to some unknown aspect of the procedure that somehow encouraged this kind of behavior. If the latter were true, it could raise a serious question about our interpretation of the data. Consequently, the chance expectation of choosing the initially less attractive alternative was computed on the basis of unreliability of the initial rating. This was done in the following way. Changes from the initial rating to the final post-decision rating were tabulated for all hair styles not involved in the choice that had been rated initially between 2 and 7 on the rating scale. In other words, we examined the changes in ratings of hair styles that were initially rated at the same levels as those used for the choice but which had themselves not been used for the choice. We could then compute the probability of a reversal occurring between any pair of ratings, that is, between a pair initially rated 2 and 3, between a pair initially rated 3 and 4, and so on. Weighting each of these probabilities according to the distribution of such pairs in the actual choices that were presented to the subject, we calculated the chance expectancy of choosing the less attractive alternative. Both conditions are virtually identical in this regard. For the no-prior-decision condition one would expect 35 per cent to choose the initially less attractive alternative simply because of unreliability of rating. The corresponding figure for the prior-decision condition is 37 per cent.

It turns out that the incidence of actually choosing the less attractive alternative in the no-prior-decision condition is fully compatible with the unreliability of the rating. Actually, it is slightly, and insignificantly, less than chance expectation. The incidence of decision reversal obtained in the prior-decision condition, on the other hand, is significantly greater than the chance level ($\chi^2 = 8.78$, significant at less than the 1 per cent level).

It will have occurred to the reader to ask about the extent to which the reversals that occurred were already apparent in the ranking that was done before the subject was expressly asked to choose. The data show that for both conditions slightly more than half of the reversals are already present in the ranking. This, however, is not a very revealing result. Many subjects, after having ranked their hair styles, went over them again, changing the rank positions of some of the styles. Many of the reversals due to post-decision regret in the prior-decision condition occurred at this point. Indeed, the fact that the procedure allowed this immediate response to the salience of dissonance probably contributed to the success of the experiment. It is of interest, however, that there was an almost total absence of "re-reversals." That is, only three subjects in the entire sample reversed from the initial rating to the ranking and then reversed again by choosing the one initially rated higher. This may indicate that the regret phenomenon is, indeed, fleeting and does not produce an unending sequence of reversal tendencies.

It is also of interest to inquire into the pattern of post-decision dissonance reduction shown by the two experimental conditions. After all, the period of salience of dissonance must be a relatively brief one in this situation and, given a little bit of time, dissonance reduction should show itself. By the time of the final post-decision rating of the hair styles one should be able to observe the usual post-decision systematic re-evaluation of alternatives.

We might expect to find a difference between the two conditions, however. In the prior-decision condition, having made their decision during the ranking, the subjects have had more time to recover from the post-decision regret and, hence, might be expected to show a larger dissonance-reduction effect by the time of the final rating. Table 5.1 presents the data for the two conditions on the initial rating and the final rating of the chosen and rejected alternatives. The last column in the table presents the usual measure of dissonance reduction, namely, increase in attractiveness of the chosen alternative plus decrease in attractiveness of the rejected alternative.

There is a problem in examining such data in this experiment that was primarily designed for a different purpose. This problem arises because of the different number of reversals in the two conditions. It is quite obvious that those who reverse, that is, who choose the initially less attractive alternative, will have appreciably larger dissonance-reduction measures than those whose choices are consistent with their initial rating. Consequently, if we simply looked at the data for each condition as a whole, there would be an effect favoring the prior-decision condition, since there were many more reversals in that condition. Table 5.1, consequently, shows the data separately for those who reversed and those who did not.

It is clear from an examination of the data that irrespective of experimental condition and of whether the choice was consistent with, or a reversal from, the original rating, there is evidence of dissonance reduction by the time of the final rating. In all cases the dissonance-reduction measures are significantly different from zero at or beyond the 5 per cent level. Also, of course, the dissonance-reduction measures are larger for the "reversal" subjects than for the "consistent" ones. This is trivial, however, since simply having the final ratings consistent in direction with the choice would produce a large number.

TABLE 5.1

Comparison of Average Initial and Final Ratings of the Chosen and Rejected Hair Styles

	Initial Rating		Final Rating		Dissonance Reduction
	Chosen	Rejected	Chosen	Rejected	
Consistent Choice					
Prior Decision					
(N = 12)	3.6	4.7	2.6	5.1	+1.4
No Prior Decision					
(N = 26)	3.5	4.6	2.9	4.8	+0.8
Reversal Choice					
Prior Decision					
(N = 20)	5.0	4.0	3.2	4.6	+2.4
No Prior Decision					
(N = 10)	4.6	3.6	3.4	3.8	+1.4

Of greater interest is the comparison between the two experimental conditions. Regardless of the direction of the choice, the subjects in the prior-decision condition show greater dissonance reduction than those in the no-prior-decision condition. However, neither the difference for the consistent choice subjects nor that for the reversal choice subjects is significant, although the latter approaches significance with a *t* of 1.51. No attempt was made to push the statistical analysis farther considering the huge difference between the two conditions in type of decision. We are content simply to accept the results as suggesting that it takes time to recover from the post-decision regret.

While the data certainly support the notion of post-decision salience of dissonance, we should examine whether or not there are plausible alternative explanations. At least one other possible explanation suggests itself. In the prior-decision condition, the effect of knowing during the ranking which two they would be asked to choose between may have been to focus attention on the two critical hair styles for a longer time and may have induced more detailed examination and consideration of these two styles. Given the fact that the initial ratings are relatively unreliable, such increased attention and consideration might have produced the obtained effect. Perhaps the more the two hair styles were considered, the more likely it would be for new considerations to enter, thus increasing the likelihood of choosing the alternative originally rated as less desirable.

In order to check on the validity of this alternative explanation, another experimental condition was run which we may call the "attention-focusing" condition. The procedure here was identical to the procedure for the other two conditions except that the step of ranking the 12 hair styles was omitted. In its place a procedure was substituted to focus the subject's attention on the two styles that were to be used for the choice. The girl was told that the company was interested in more detailed descriptions, and more detailed reactions, to a few of the hair styles. She was handed one of the photographs and asked to comment in detail on it. She was then handed another and was similarly encouraged to react to it in detail. Altogether, four photographs were thus commented on. At the conclusion of these descriptions, she was given the same "information" as in the other experimental conditions and was asked to make a choice between two of the hair styles that she had reacted to in detail. In short, in this condition the subjects did not make any prior decisions but had their attention focused on detailed consideration of the alternatives that they were later to choose between.

Nineteen girls were run in this condition. Four out of the 19 (21 per cent) chose the alternative that they had originally rated as less attractive. Clearly, the alternative explanation is not valid. At least in this situation, focusing attention and detailed consideration did not induce a greater number of reversals.

Since the attention-focusing condition was run later than the other two experimental conditions, we also, at the same time, assigning subjects at random, ran seven additional girls each in the no-prior-decision and the prior-decision conditions, simply to be sure that the effect we had obtained was still operating. Although the number of cases here is too small for statistical significance to show itself, the results closely duplicate what had previously been obtained in these conditions. In the no-prior-decision condition, two out of the seven girls (29 per cent) chose the less attractive hair style. In the prior-decision condition, four out of the seven (57 per cent) showed decision reversal.

Summary

Two experimental conditions were run in order to test a hypothesis concerning post-decision salience of dissonance. Girls were given a choice of which of two hair styles they wanted for a free hair setting. In one condition the subjects had already made a "decision" by ranking one as more desirable than the other before they were asked to indicate their choice. In the other condition no decision had been made before they were asked, formally, to make one. It was reasoned that in the former condition, post-decision regret would exist when they were asked to make their choice, and that this would be reflected in a high incidence of decision reversals.

The data support this hypothesis concerning post-decision regret. In the prior-decision condition there were significantly more decision reversals than in the no-prior-decision condition. In order to make sure that this result was not obtained because of different amounts of attention paid to the alternatives, another experimental condition was subsequently run. No prior decision was made in this additional condition, but the subjects were induced to give a lot of attention to the hair styles that were to be involved in the choice. The incidence of decision reversal was quite low in this condition. It seems plausible to maintain that following a decision there is a sudden salience of dissonance that is experienced as regret about the decision.

■

It is fair to say that, considering the results of the Festinger and Walster experiment, we have some evidence that there does occur a period of post-decision regret. But how compelling is this evidence? In general, there are two things that affect the extent to which certain data compel us toward a specific theoretical interpretation. The first, and the most important, is the availability of alternative explanations that are equally good or better. It is, indeed, difficult to think of adequate alternative explanations for the results of the Festinger and Walster experiment and, to this extent, the data seem reasonably compelling. There is, however, a second factor. Although it may be difficult, or even impossible, to construct an adequate alternative explanation immediately, one may have various degrees of confidence that a better alternative interpretation will soon be invented. If such a belief is strong, one usually does not regard the data as compelling, regardless of the current dearth of alternative explanations.

Let us examine the Festinger and Walster experiment from this point of view. Although it is rather straightforward and simple from a methodological point of view, it is a highly complicated experiment from a theoretical point of view. The interpretation in terms of post-decision regret rests upon the assumption that once a person knows that he will be asked to choose between two alternatives, the action of ranking these two, together with several others, forces him to make a decision between them. It further assumes that such a "decision," even though it is not a formal one, and even though it is clearly revocable, initiates the same post-decision processes as an actual choice. These assumptions, inherent in the "regret" interpretation of the experiment, may turn out to be questionable.

Another problem exists also. The Festinger and Walster experiment does not have a direct measure reflecting post-decision regret. Instead, the experiment relies on the reasoning that if a sufficiently large number of people experience a sufficiently large magnitude of post-decision regret, then we will observe a large enough frequency of actual decision reversal. The measure employed, namely, the relative frequency of choosing the alternative originally rated as less attractive, is a rather indirect measure. In short, because of the assumptions involved in interpreting the procedure, and because of the indirectness of the dependent variable, the results are not very compelling with respect to the hypothesis about salience of dissonance.

Certainly, a more direct test of the hypothesis should be possible. If there is a temporary period of regret following a decision because of immediate post-decision salience of dissonance, one should be able to observe directly that at some point, soon after the decision, the chosen alternative has become less attractive and the rejected alternative has become more attractive. One should also be able to observe that this phase of the post-decision process is followed by dissonance reduction and the spreading apart of the attractiveness of the alternatives. If one could show this directly in an experiment, it would certainly lend considerable weight to the whole idea of post-decision regret.

There are obvious difficulties connected with doing such an experiment in the laboratory. Probably, in order to demonstrate the temporal sequence of regret followed by dissonance reduction, one requires a situation in which the post-decision dissonance is very large, the decision very important, and dissonance reduction rather difficult. In this type of situation it seems reasonable to suppose that the immediate post-decision salience of dissonance would be marked enough to show itself clearly in ratings and, if dissonance reduction is difficult, the regret would last for a long enough time to be measurable. It is clearly not easy to construct this kind of decision situation in the laboratory. The experiment reported next by Walster represents a compromise between the laboratory and real life. It is a rather successful attempt to use an important, real decision in a relatively controlled manner for experimental purposes.

Experiment
The Temporal Sequence of Post-Decision Processes

Elaine Walster

This experiment was performed in order to obtain evidence bearing directly on the hypothesis that immediately following a decision there is a temporary period in which the person experiences regret. The clearest and most direct way in which this hypothesis can be examined is to have subjects make a decision and then to remeasure the attractiveness of the alternatives at varying intervals of time following the decision. If the regret phenomenon occurs, one should find that in a period soon after the decision the chosen alternative becomes *less* attractive and the rejected alternative *more* attractive than they had been before the decision. After this, of course, if the theory is correct, one would obtain the usual evidence of dissonance reduction.

The consideration of such a design, however, brings us face to face with a difficult problem. There have been many studies concerned with post-decision dissonance reduction, all of which have remeasured the attractiveness of the alternatives very soon after the decision. They have all yielded evidence that dissonance reduction occurs. Clearly, if we are to maintain the hypothesis about the regret period in the face of the evidence from these experiments, we are forced to contend that, at least in those experiments, the regret period was very fleeting indeed. The question of design then becomes: How can we construct a decision situation in which the regret phase in the post-decision process is relatively long-lasting?

If one examines the characteristic situation used in previous experiments, some clues concerning the answer to this question may be obtained. Typically, these experiments have presented subjects with a choice between two alternatives, both of which were positive in nature and possessed no negative attributes at all. If a person is offered a choice between two phonograph records as a gift, for example, even if one of them is not very well liked, there is nothing negative about having it. At a minimum, if the person does not like the gift he gets, he can throw it away and he is no worse off than before. In addition, of course, the decision is not a very important one for the person. It has few consequences of any lasting nature for him. It seems reasonable to conjecture that in this kind of situation dissonance reduction proceeds very rapidly and regret is very momentary.

The attempt was made, consequently, to find a situation in which subjects could be offered a decision between alternatives that had both positive and negative aspects, that would be reasonably important to the subject, and in which the decision would have lasting consequences. Furthermore, one would want to be able to employ this decision situation in a well-controlled context. It would be necessary to measure the attractiveness of the alternatives before the decision and, assigning subjects to conditions at random, remeasure the attractiveness at different lengths of time after the decision. One would also want to control the activity of the subject and his interactions with others during the entire period between initial measurement and final measurement.

Fortunately, we were able to obtain the cooperation of the Sixth Army District Reception Center at Fort Ord, California. Arrangements were made to use as subjects in the experiment men who were drafted into the Army. They were each to be given a choice of which of two occupational specialties they wanted to be assigned to for their two years in the service. Certainly, such a decision, affecting two years of their lives, is reasonably important; the descriptions of the occupational specialties could be written so as to emphasize both positive and negative aspects of each alternative; and dissonance reduction in this situation should not be a particularly easy affair. In short, this seemed a reasonable situation for testing the validity of the hypothesis about post-decision regret. The details of, and the reasons for, the experimental procedure are given below.

Procedure

Two hundred and seventy-seven draftees who reported for processing at the Fort Ord Reception Center were used as subjects. Each subject was run in the experiment within a day or two of his arrival at the Reception Center—before he had gone far enough in his initial processing to have any information about his probable job assignment in the Army. Men who had enlisted, or who for any other reason had something to say about their job assignment, were excluded from the sample. Men were made available for the experiment on weekends and on days when there were so many arrivals at the Reception Center that not all of them could be processed. In this way, the study did not interfere with the normal processing activity at the Reception Center, nor did it prolong the time any man spent there.

The Army personnel were asked to select men to assign to the study who had had at least some high school education but who had not completed college. It was felt that the job selections to be offered would be most appropriate for men with intermediate education. Frequently, however, information on educational level was not available to the Army personnel at the time they assigned men to the study and so this selection on educational criteria was not rigorous. In our total sample, six subjects had had no high school education at all and fifteen had completed college.

Early in the course of running the experiment it was realized that most of the alien draftees and many of the Spanish-speaking men had difficulty understanding the instructions and had trouble in making the ratings required of them. Consequently, we requested the Army personnel to exclude such subjects in the future.

Nineteen Spanish-speaking and four alien draftees who had already been run in the experiment were discarded from the sample.

Five subjects at a time were run through the experiment. A uniformed driver met the five men at the Reception Center and drove them to the experimental building, about ten minutes away. During the drive he told them that they had been randomly selected for a special job placement program that the Army was conducting and that they would receive a definite job assignment some time during the day. The driver also commented that although the jobs the special placement program had to offer were, perhaps, not as good as those they might have in civilian life, they were better than those the men could hope to get under the regular job placement program. These comments were intended to make the men believe that, whatever job they were assigned that day, it was definite and as good as or better than anything else they could get.

As soon as the driver arrived at the experimental building, he assembled the men and introduced them to the two experimenters standing in the doorway.

Experimenter 1 then explained to the men:

As he has probably told you, we're working for the Army on a special experimental program of job placement. You were more or less randomly selected from men in your educational category. Today, I'm going to interview each one of you. I can only see one of you at a time, so while you're waiting for your interview, Miss Turner (Experimenter 2) will be getting some other necessary information from you. She'll ask you to fill out some questionnaires concerning the kind of jobs you've held, the things you like and dislike in a job, and so forth.

O.K. [*Pointing to the closest man*] I'll be seeing you first. Miss Turner will tell the rest of you what to do.

The first subject was then led into the large room where Experimenter 1 conducted all the interviewing. Experimenter 2 took each of the other four men to separate small cubicles in the experimental building. When all four men had been seated, Experimenter 2 distributed Questionnaire 1 which asked the men about their previous job and educational experience.

At the same time, in the main experimental room, Experimenter 1 asked the first subject to be seated. On the table in front of the subject's chair was a large chart titled "How Much Would You Like to Work at This Job in the Army for the Next Two Years?"

Underneath the title was a 31-point scale. The highest point on the scale (Point 1) was labeled "Would like extremely much." Point 31 was labeled "Would dislike extremely much."

Experimenter 1 then explained to the subject:

Today we're interested in getting a fairly precise idea of how attractive a number of jobs that the Army is especially interested in seem to you. So, I'll tell you a little bit more about 10 different jobs. I'd like you to think about these jobs and decide how much you'd like to work at each one during your next two years in the Army. Do take into account all those personal things and preferences that make you want one job more than another. You will be assigned to one of these jobs, and I'll be able to tell you which one you got before you leave today.

To help you to give us a pretty clear idea of how you feel about each of these jobs, we've made up this scale.

The scale on the chart was then explained to the subject; some civilian job titles, printed on arrow-shaped cards, were placed at various points on the scale by the experimenter to demonstrate further how the scale was to be used. At this point, the subject was encouraged to ask questions.

Experimenter 1 then picked up a packet of 10 arrow-shaped cards, each having an Army job title and job description printed on it. She told the subject:

Now whichever of these jobs you're assigned to, you will have to go to school for from six to eight weeks to learn how to do that job in the Army manner.

Now I'll read the job description that's printed on each arrow along with you. Then take your time and decide how much you like each job, and then put the arrow at the right spot. If you should change your mind as we go along, and feel that some job should be rated higher or lower, naturally, it's all right to change that job's position. However, it's probably a good idea to reread the description of the job you're thinking of changing, because sometimes the reason you think you've made a mistake is that you've forgotten some of the things that are involved in the job.

Take as much time as you want. We're anxious to get a really accurate idea both of how much you like each job relative to the others, and how much you like each job absolutely; that is, exactly at which of the points on the scale you think it belongs.

Experimenter 1 then read the 10 job titles and descriptions to the subject, pausing after each description so the subject could place a titled arrow at the appropriate point on the scale.

These job descriptions were written so that each job appeared to have a few really desirable and a few really undesirable features. It was hoped that this obvious mixture of good and bad elements in each job would increase the amount of dissonance subjects experienced and make dissonance reduction more difficult.

When the subject had finished placing all 10 job arrows, the experimenter suggested:

Now that you've seen all the jobs, it's probably a good idea to reread the job descriptions and make sure you get everything just where you want it. Sometimes we just can't give you the jobs you like most, and so we'd like to know how you feel about every one of the jobs.

When this subject had finished his final ratings of the jobs, Experimenter 1 took him to a separate cubicle and then returned to the large experimental room to record where on the 31-point scale he had rated each of the 10 jobs. This initial interview usually took 12 to 15 minutes.

Experimenter 1 then called in the second subject from his cubicle to the large experimental room and followed a procedure identical to that followed for the first subject. At the same time, Experimenter 2 asked Subject 1 to fill out Questionnaire 1, which the other subjects had completed earlier, and asked Subjects 3 through 5 to fill out Questionnaire 2.

Approximately every 15 minutes another subject was interviewed by Experimenter 1 and the remaining subjects were given the next in a series of four questionnaires to fill out. The purpose of these questionnaires was primarily to keep the subject occupied while Experimenter 1 was interviewing the other men. Also, the questionnaires, taken from material contained in the subtests of the Strong Vocational Interest Inventory, helped make the later job selection seem more plausible.

Subjects filled out questionnaires and were interviewed according to the following sequence:

Time Schedule	Subject 1	Subject 2	Subject 3	Subject 4	Subject 5
1st 15 min.	Interview	Ques. 1	Ques. 1	Ques. 1	Ques. 1
2nd 15 min.	Ques. 1	Interview	Ques. 2	Ques. 2	Ques. 2
3rd 15 min.	Ques. 2	Ques. 2	Interview	Ques. 3	Ques. 3
4th 15 min.	Ques. 3	Ques. 3	Ques. 3	Interview	Ques. 4
5th 15 min.	Ques. 4	Ques. 4	Ques. 4	Ques. 4	Interview

The purpose of the initial interview was to obtain a measure of how each subject evaluated each job before he was faced with a decision. The next step was to select two jobs and to offer the subject a choice between them. Ideally, it would have been desirable to offer each subject a choice between jobs that he had rated near the middle of the scale, with the initial ratings separated by a constant amount and identical for all subjects. To approach this as closely as possible without discarding too many subjects, Experimenter 2 examined the initial ratings of each subject and selected the two jobs he should be offered according to the following criteria:

1. The job the subject liked best was never used as one of the alternatives for choice. Similarly, none of the three least attractive jobs was used. When possible, the next to the most attractive job was also avoided.

2. No job rated above 6 on the attractiveness scale ("Would like very much") or below 18 (between "Would like and dislike equally" and "Would dislike fairly much") was ever offered as one of the two choice alternatives.

3. Within the above restrictions, two jobs were selected to offer the subject that were rated approximately five units apart on the 31-point scale. If there were no two jobs rated five units apart that satisfied the other criteria, jobs rated six units apart were used. If this too were not possible, jobs rated four units apart, seven units apart, or three units apart were used.

If none of these conditions could be met, the subject was not used in the experiment. Altogether, ten subjects were discarded because no pair of jobs could be offered them under the above set of restrictions.

After Experimenter 2 had made the selection of which jobs should be offered to each subject, Experimenter 1 called the first subject back into the experimental room.

She stated:

Well, by now we can give you some definite information about your Army assignment for the next two years. We've examined all the preferences you expressed to me, the scores on the tests you took for Miss Turner, and considered your background information and job experience.

You understand that in the Army, job assignment is in large part determined by what jobs the Army has to fill at any given time. In this experimental job placement program, we are trying to work out a really good compromise between what you can do, what you want to do, and what jobs we have to fill. The very best we can do for you, considering your test scores and the Army's needs, is to offer you a choice between these two jobs.

Experimenter 1 then handed the subject the arrows (containing job titles and job descriptions) for the two jobs between which he was to decide and reread the descriptions to him.

Experimenter 1 then concluded: "As soon as you decide which of the two jobs you want, tell me. I can definitely assign you to whichever one you choose for your time in the Army."

If the subject asked why he had not been offered the job he ranked first in the initial interview, Experimenter 1 told him that the main determinant could have been his test scores, the Army's current needs, or the qualifications of the other draftees. For specific information he was told that he would have to see Miss Turner. It was stressed, however, that these were the only jobs available to him.

Subjects were randomly assigned to one of four experimental conditions, the only difference between the conditions being the interval of time allowed to elapse between the decision and the remeasurement of the attractiveness of the jobs. One-fourth of the subjects rerated the jobs immediately after the decision. The others rerated the jobs after an interval of four minutes, 15 minutes, or 90 minutes.

If the subject was assigned to the "Immediate Condition," the experimenter continued:

O.K. There are a couple of other things I'd like you to do. The next thing I'd like you to do will in no way affect your Army assignment, but it will help us in developing and improving our job placement program.

By now you've had quite a bit of time to think about these jobs [*pointing to the 10 jobs*], and jobs in general, and you've probably thought of a lot of things that make a job good or bad that just didn't occur to you before. What we'd like you to do is to rerate all these jobs now that you've had a reasonable length of time to think about them.

The subject was then handed a 10-page questionnaire, each page exactly like the chart on which he had rated the jobs during his first interview.

Experimenter 1 continued:

The scale they've provided is just like the one you used earlier, only there's a separate rating page for each job. If you'd write the job number up at the top of each page, we'd know which one you are talking about. Then just draw an arrow at that place which most accurately represents how you feel about each job, *right at this moment.*

If the subject had been assigned to the four-minute, 15-minute, or 90-minute condition, then, after saying "O.K. There are a couple of other things I'd like you to do," Experimenter 1 added, "but there's some work I have to do first. If you'd just wait 'right here' (four-minute condition), or 'across the hall in your room' (15-minute and 90-minute conditions), I'll get back to you just as soon as I can. Sometimes it takes quite a while. Don't worry, I haven't forgotten you." The experimenter then left the subject alone with nothing to do for the appropriate number of minutes.

When Experimenter 1 returned (after four minutes, 15 minutes, or 90 minutes), she followed the same procedure described for the immediate condition.

Results

If the phenomenon of post-decision regret is a real one, and if evidence of it exists in this experiment, it should be reflected in a drawing together of the two alternatives soon after the decision is made. That is, sometime in the immediate post-decision period the chosen alternative should *decrease* in attractiveness and the rejected alternative *increase* in attractiveness. This, of course, should be followed by the usual spreading apart of the alternatives that is the normal evidence of dissonance reduction.

The experiment was designed in ignorance, of course, of the time interval at which post-decision regret would be at its maximum. That is, it was theoretically conceivable that regret would be seen as soon as the decision was made. It was also theoretically conceivable that it could take a little time before the regret would develop to measurable quantities. For this reason we included an immediate condition, a four-minute-delay condition, and a 15-minute-delay condition. Conceivably, it could take as long as 15 minutes, or even longer, for regret to develop. We simply did not know ahead of time. The 90-minute condition was included to make sure that we had at least one interval long enough for recovery from regret to occur and for the effects of dissonance reduction to be evident. The interval of 90 minutes was chosen as the longest time that it seemed at all feasible to keep a person sitting alone in a small room with nothing to do but wait.

Before we look at the data, there is one decision that must be made about the analysis. Of the 244 subjects from whom usable data were obtained, 51 (21 per cent), when asked to make a choice, chose the job that they had originally rated as the *less* attractive of the two they were offered. This is, of course, a rather high percentage of such inversions. In any experiment of this type a certain number of inversions will occur because new considerations of a major character occur to the subject between the time of making the rating and the time of making the decision. There are also, usually, some subjects who make the ratings on a rather abstract basis, but who, when faced with the decision, suddenly consider the alternatives in a new light of reality. In addition to this, in the current experiment there were undoubtedly many subjects who simply did not understand the rating scale fully, some who did not listen to or did not adequately comprehend the job descriptions, and some who were simply not interested. It must be remembered that the subjects comprised a very heterogeneous population, many of them being run through the experiment on the very first day that they reported to the Army Reception Center.

Whatever the reasons for the inversions, they represent a difficulty for analysis. It represents something of a distortion to disregard them or simply to throw them together for analysis with data from other subjects. Since there are so many subjects who show inversions, their data will be presented separately. Since these subjects come about equally from all conditions, this does not interfere with any comparison among the four conditions and, by presenting their data separately, we can determine whether they show the same trends as the other subjects. The data for the 193 subjects who chose the alternative they had rated as *more* attractive will be presented first, and then the other data will be examined for comparison.

Table 5.2 presents the data on ratings of the chosen and rejected alternatives for the major portion of the sample, namely, those who chose the job they had originally rated as more desirable. The first two columns of figures show the pre-decision ratings of the

TABLE 5.2

Mean Ratings of Chosen and Rejected Alternatives for
Subjects Who Chose the More Attractive Job

Experimental Condition	Pre-Decision Ratings		Change from Pre-Decision to Post-Decision Ratings		Change in Discrepancy
	Chosen	Rejected	Chosen	Rejected	
Immediate (N = 48)	9.80	15.09	.70	.00	.71
Four Minutes (N = 48)	9.79	15.02	−.37	−.97	−1.34
Fifteen Minutes (N = 48)	10.04	14.98	1.56	.58	2.14
Ninety Minutes (N = 49)	9.91	14.84	.67	−.36	.31

NOTE: Change scores are indicated as positive if they are in the direction of dissonance reduction and as negative if they are in the opposite direction. Thus, changes toward greater attractiveness of the chosen alternative and toward less attractiveness of the rejected alternative are scored as positive changes.

two alternatives. It is, of course, no surprise that these figures are so similar from condition to condition, since there were rather narrow limits within which the two jobs offered could have been rated and, in addition, subjects were assigned to conditions at random. The third and fourth columns of figures show the changes from the pre-decision to the post-decision ratings of each alternative. The last column shows the total amount of dissonance reduction that occurred.

A glance at the figures in this last column of Table 5.2 shows that there is, indeed, a period of post-decision regret followed by appreciable dissonance reduction. In the condition in which the alternatives were rerated immediately after the decision, there is a relatively small change of .71 in the direction of dissonance reduction, a change that is not significantly different from zero ($t = 1.38$). Those subjects who rerated the jobs after a four-minute delay period show the opposite of dissonance reduction, namely, regret. In this condition the chosen alternative decreases somewhat in attractiveness while the rejected alternative increases in attractiveness. The total change of -1.34 is significantly different from zero at the 7 per cent level ($t = 1.80$) and significantly different from the change obtained in the immediate condition at the 2 per cent level ($t = 2.26$).

It does, then, seem that in this experiment evidence of post-decision regret exists and that it takes a little time for this regret phenomenon to show itself. If one examines the data for those subjects who rerated the jobs after a delay of 15 minutes, one observes, furthermore, that the period of post-decision regret is, indeed, a temporary one. After 15 post-decision minutes have elapsed there is no more evidence of regret but rather clear evidence of the usual dissonance reduction. By this time the chosen alternative is rated as more attractive and the rejected alternative as less attractive than they were initially. The total change of 2.14 is significantly different from zero ($t = 2.90$) and from the four-minute condition ($t = 3.32$). It is clear that we did, indeed, obtain post-decision regret followed by dissonance reduction. The various experimental conditions are significantly different from one another in a clear and unequivocal manner. For example, an analysis of variance on all four experimental conditions yields an F of 3.99, which, for three and 189 degrees of freedom, is significant beyond the 1 per cent level.

The data for the 90-minute-delay condition, however, provide a rather surprising result. Instead of continuing to obtain dissonance reduction equal to or greater than that obtained in the 15-minute-delay condition, one finds that after 90 minutes have elapsed there is no evidence of any dissonance reduction at all. The change of $.31$ is not significantly different from zero and, because of increased variability in this condition, is not clearly different from either the 15-minute condition ($t = 1.69$) or the four-minute condition ($t = 1.52$). It is difficult to understand this result, although there are some good hunches that can be offered. We will, however, postpone our discussion of the perplexing 90-minute condition temporarily.

Let us first turn our attention to the data obtained from those subjects who chose the job they had initially rated as the less attractive of the two they were offered. These data are presented in Table 5.3. It is clear from a glance at the last column in the table, which presents the total change in discrepancy between the

TABLE 5.3

Mean Ratings of Chosen and Rejected Alternatives for Subjects Who Chose the Less Attractive Job

Experimental Condition	Pre-Decision Ratings		Change from Pre-Decision to Post-Decision Ratings		Change in Discrepancy
	Chosen	Rejected	Chosen	Rejected	
Immediate (N = 12)	14.78	10.18	4.70	2.03	6.73
Four minutes (N = 13)	14.93	10.62	1.58	3.53	5.11
Fifteen Minutes (N = 13)	14.46	10.03	3.50	3.62	7.12
Ninety Minutes (N = 13)	15.04	10.56	2.99	2.44	5.43

two alternatives, that the absolute magnitude of these changes is very large. Undoubtedly, this is simply a reflection of the fact that for these subjects the initial rating is relatively meaningless. For these data one must simply ignore the absolute magnitude of the results and look just at the comparison among conditions. It may be seen that the results go in exactly the same direction as the previous results we discussed. From the immediate condition to the four-minute condition the change in discrepancy decreases, from four minutes to 15 minutes it increases, and by 90 minutes it has decreased again. The numbers of cases are rather small, and the variability for these subjects is quite large. None of these differences is statistically significant. The only point to be made is that these subjects show largely the same pattern of results as the others, even duplicating the perplexing problem of the 90-minute condition.

What are some of the possible reasons for the results from the 90-minute condition? The first inclination, on obtaining a result that is so surprising from a theoretical point of view, is to suspect some purely technical methodological inadequacy. In this particular experiment there is a natural inclination to suspect that in the 90-minute condition, the very long period of sitting alone in a small room with nothing to do may have introduced boredom, anger, resentment, or any of a number of other factors that might have contributed to the obtained result. This may or may not be true, but the best judgment we can make is that it is not true. Let us look closely at some aspects of the "boredom" explanation to see why this judgment seems reasonable.

It is conceivable that after 90 minutes of sitting along in a small room, these subjects felt angry with the Army. This experience may have confirmed all their worst expectations, with the result that they may have felt that everything in the Army is terrible, including the possible jobs. If this explanation had any validity at all, we would expect that the average post-decision rating of the jobs not involved in the choice would be considerably lower for subjects in the 90-minute-delay condition than for subjects in the other conditions. This, however, is not the case. The average post-decision ratings of the jobs not involved in the choice were 15.89, 15.35, 15.51, and 15.51 for the four conditions—differences which are certainly indistinguishable from one another.

Another possible aspect of the "boredom" explanation is that being bored and having lost interest in the whole proceedings, the subjects in the 90-minute-delay condition stop discriminating among jobs on the post-decision ratings. That is, out of boredom or, perhaps, anger, they make their second ratings in a perfunctory manner, essentially saying that everything is the same. To check on this possibility we computed the standard deviation of each subject's post-decision ratings of the jobs. If they stopped cooperating and stopped discriminating among jobs, we would expect this to be reflected in a smaller dispersion of the individual's ratings. This again is not true. The four conditions are almost identical.

Nowhere could any evidence be found to support a contention of methodological inadequacy in the 90-minute condition. Consequently, we have come to the conclusion that it is probably a real effect. But if it is a real effect, what does it mean? Is dissonance reduction just a temporary matter? This seems unlikely. Although there has been little done concerning long-range effects of dissonance reduction, what we do know would certainly argue against the disappearance of all effects within 90 minutes. Ninety minutes may be a long time to sit doing nothing in a room but, after all,

it is a short amount of time in which to expect a rather pervasive
process to be completely nullified.

This still, however, leaves us with no answer to the perplexing
result of the 90-minute condition. And we can give no good answer
—not in the sense of an answer that can be supported with data.
We can, however, offer what seems to us to be a good hunch. We
think the answer lies in the great difficulty of reducing dissonance
in this experimental situation. Let us look at this more carefully.
In choosing this particular context for doing this experiment, we
were motivated primarily by our intuitive notions concerning the
conditions under which regret would be rather pronounced and
would last for a sufficiently long time so that we could measure it.
Intuitively, it seemed to us that this would happen if the decision
were important, the alternatives possessed a mixture of good and
bad characteristics, and dissonance reduction was very difficult.
The idea was that under such circumstances the post-decision dissonance would be large and, if dissonance reduction were difficult
and took time, that focusing on the dissonance in order to reduce
it would produce the regret phase. If dissonance reduction were
too easy, the regret phase might be very fleeting.

We were probably very successful in creating a situation in
which dissonance reduction was, indeed, difficult. At least we
know that we did obtain a period in which post-decision regret
appeared. We probably created a situation in which only a limited
amount of dissonance could be reduced by most subjects. Under
most ordinary "real-life" circumstances, the person would go talk
to others about it, seek new information, and generally try to get
informational and social support for the process of further reducing dissonance. In our experiment this was impossible. The person
was left entirely on his own resources. There was no new information obtainable and there was no one else he could even talk to
about it. It is possible that after some dissonance had been reduced,
the continued focusing on the remaining dissonance without further successful dissonance reduction could produce the effect obtained in the 90-minute condition.

If this is the correct explanation, there are certain implications.
If one were to set up a situation in which dissonance reduction
was even more difficult, almost impossible, the effect of focusing
on and unsuccessfully trying to reduce the dissonance might result
in a steady increase in the importance of the dissonance and a

steady narrowing of the discrepancy between the alternatives. If in our experimental situation the subjects had been provided with more leeway, people to talk to, things to read about the Army and its jobs—anything that would have aided dissonance reduction— the results of the 90-minute condition might have been different.

Summary

An experiment was conducted to test the hypothesis that:

1. Shortly after having made a decision, the subject, because of the salience of dissonance, will experience a period in which the chosen alternative seems less attractive and the rejected alternative more attractive than they were prior to the decision.

2. This "regret" period will be followed by the customary dissonance-reduction process and the spreading apart of the alternatives in terms of attractiveness.

The subjects in the experiment had to make a decision that was rather important and would affect two years of their lives. Reratings of alternatives were obtained immediately after the decision for some subjects, four minutes afterward for some, 15 minutes afterward for others, and 90 minutes afterward for still others.

The data showed clear evidence of "regret" four minutes after the decision. Fifteen minutes after the decision, recovery had occurred and there was clear evidence of dissonance reduction. Surprising results were obtained from those subjects measured 90 minutes after the decision. There was no evidence here of any dissonance reduction.

■

We may come to the conclusion that at least under some conditions there is a measurable period of post-decision regret. Indirect evidence of this, in the form of post-decision reversal of choice, was obtained in the Festinger and Walster experiment, and very direct evidence was obtained in the Walster experiment. The two sets of data, taken together, certainly make the conclusion very plausible.

The ideas behind both of the experiments that were reported in this chapter may be summarized very briefly. It seems likely that immediately after a decision the person focuses his attention on the dissonance that exists in an attempt to reduce it. The person examines the dissonant relations, tries to think them through, and tries to convince himself of things that will increase consonance. After all, how else can we expect dissonance to be reduced other than by focusing on, and trying to do something about, the dissonant relations?

It seems likely, furthermore, that one effect of focusing on the dissonance that exists would be to make that dissonance loom larger and seem more important. It is for this reason that we are led to expect a period in which post-decision regret is obtained. How severe and how long in duration the regret period is would be determined by how quickly dissonance can be reduced. If dissonance were easy to reduce and were reduced readily and in large amounts, the regret period might be insignificant and very fleeting. If dissonance were difficult to reduce, the regret period might be strong and of long duration.

At any rate, if and when enough dissonance was reduced to produce recovery from the regret period, we certainly expected to observe stable dissonance reduction. To have observed, as we did in the Walster experiment, a period of regret followed by post-decision dissonance reduction, followed by a diminution in the amount of measurable dissonance reduction, is unexpected and requires more consideration.

The major explanation suggested by Walster is simply that if dissonance reduction is almost impossible beyond a certain amount, and if the subject keeps focusing on the dissonance and keeps trying, unsuccessfully, to reduce it, this will produce an increase in importance of the dissonance that remains. The increased importance of the dissonant relations, in the absence of further dissonance reduction, may produce the effects obtained in the 90-minute-delay condition. At first glance this explanation seems very forced and complicated, perhaps so complicated as to make it unpalatable. It may, however, be correct. It is quite possible that precisely those conditions which produce a measurable regret phenomenon also produce instability of the dissonance reduction in a situation where external aids to dissonance reduction are unavailable. Only future research will tell. It is clearly important to have data concerning the long-range effects of dissonance-reducing processes.

Chapter Six

Aspects of the Pre-Decision Cognitive Process

■

In Chapter 1 we remarked that in spite of long-standing concern with the problem of conflict and decision making, psychologists have contributed little to an understanding of the cognitive process during the decision-making period. At this point, we must face the fact that the studies reported thus far in this volume have not contributed much to an understanding of this process either.

What have we said about the pre-decision process? It has been demonstrated that the pre-decision period is *not* characterized by a systematic process of spreading the alternatives apart in terms of attractiveness. This, however, is a rather negative kind of contribution—it does not tell us what *does* characterize the pre-decision cognitive process. The only constructive suggestion that has been made is that the pre-decision period is characterized by objective, impartial gathering and evaluation of information about the alternatives involved in the choice. This seems plausible, and some data we have presented tend to support such an assertion. But surely this is not the only thing that occurs during the process of making a decision. If it were, the decision-making process would be a rather orderly affair. The decision maker would simply collect and evaluate information about the various alternatives. As soon as he had collected and evaluated enough information so that he was relatively certain that more information would not alter the preference order that existed, he would make his decision.

Intuitively, however, it seems clear that the decision-making process is not that simple. Other factors certainly enter. Although we are very far from being able to offer any coherent account of everything that occurs, or that may occur, in the pre-decision period, we can present some theoretical and experimental exploration of two other factors that seem possibly important.

There is one obvious limitation on the idea that impartial collecting of information about the alternatives is an adequate description of the pre-decision process. For such a description to be adequate, all the alternatives in a decision situation would have to be clearly defined. Although it is certainly possible to construct laboratory decision situations in which they are so defined, it is probably rarely the case in actual decision situations. The more usual decision situation, while involving some alternatives that are clearly defined, also allows the person to search for, or to invent, new alternatives that may perhaps be more satisfactory to him than any of those which are immediately apparent.

If this is true, then a goodly portion of the time that a person spends making a decision may actually be spent not in collecting and evaluating information, but in trying to discover new alternatives or in thinking about better alternatives that are not actually available to him. He may even spend considerable time trying to devise a way to make better but unavailable alternatives actually available. For example, consider the hypothetical case of a student who has just received his Ph.D and has received job offers from two universities. Let us imagine that one job offers him a higher salary but that the other offers him a lighter teaching load. Let us further imagine that both of these jobs are very attractive to him, but that neither is a complete fulfillment of some image he has of the "ideal job." How does he go about making his decision?

Certainly, he will collect and evaluate all kinds of information about these two jobs and will spend time considering and trying to balance teaching load against salary. But we wish to suggest here that these will not be the only cognitive processes in which he engages. Many other alternatives will suggest themselves to him and he will spend considerable time thinking about, and exploring, aspects of the situation which, in a sense, are irrelevant to the decision he must make. Certainly, he can hope that some third job, even better than either of the two he has been offered, will become available. Even when he eventually disposes of this possiblity as unrealistic, there are still other alternatives that he can consider. If job A with its high salary only had less teaching connected with it, he would accept it; or if job B with its lighter teaching load only paid more money, that job would clearly be preferable. He may even go so far as to contemplate proposing such modifications to the jobs he has been offered. It seems likely that only after he has given up the idea of any of these unavailable alternatives, will he be able to decide between the two jobs.

If such processes commonly occur in decision making, it should be possible to obtain evidence about them in a controlled experimental situation. What one would want in such an experiment would be to put subjects into a relatively simple, straightforward decision situation with clearly defined alternatives. One would then want to manipulate, in a manner which in and of itself would not affect decision time, the likelihood of the person's inventing other alternatives. Measurements of decision time, and indications of what the person had been thinking about while making the decision, should then provide evidence concerning the validity of the above suggestions. Such an experiment, by Walster and Festinger, follows.

Experiment
Decisions Among Imperfect Alternatives

Elaine Walster and Leon Festinger

Does a person, when faced with a choice among imperfect although attractive alternatives, spend time thinking about more attractive possibilities that are not really available? If this does happen, then it is likely to be a feature of many decision-making situations and it would be well to understand more about it. The present experiment was designed to ascertain, in rather preliminary fashion, whether or not such a process could be observed to occur.

In order to do an experiment to ascertain whether such a hypothesized process does indeed occur, one must be somewhat more specific about the details of this process and about its measurable manifestations. One manifestation should be very clear. To the extent that a decision maker considers unavailable "ideal alternatives" and must dispose of these cognitively before making his decision, the total time it takes to make the decision should be longer. In short, if one were to compare an experimental condition in which the person did consider unavailable alternatives with a condition in which the person did not, the decision time in the former condition should be longer.

The other manifestations of this hypothesized process that one can easily specify a *priori* are concerned with the actual content of the cognition of the decision maker at various times in the process of making his decision. Early in the decision process one would expect to see evidence that the person was thinking about unavailable alternatives. By the end of the decision-making process, however, the picture should be different. If it is necessary for the person to accept the unavailability of the "ideal alternatives" and to stop thinking about them before he can make his decision, then by the end of the process of decision making one should be able to obtain evidence that he *has* stopped thinking about them.

One other problem must be solved before a fruitful experiment can be done to test the validity of this suggestion about the pre-decision process. One must find a way to manipulate experimental conditions so that in one condition it is rather likely that "ideal" but unavailable alternatives will occur to the subject, while in another condition it is less likely. Considering the exploratory nature of this investigation, we chose the most direct and least ambiguous way to do this that occurred to us. In order to encourage and facilitate thinking about very good but unavailable alternatives, we would simply have present, in this experimental condition, a very good but unavailable alternative.

The basic design of the experiment was, then, quite simple. All subjects were to be given a choice among attractive but imperfect alternatives. In one condition they would first be shown a "perfect" alternative that was not available to them. In the other condition, to keep the procedure as constant as possible, they would first be shown a worse alternative that was not available to them. We would then compare these two conditions with respect to decision time and to the content of the cognition of the subjects.

Given such a design, it is always possible that differences between these two conditions could stem from the mere presence or absence of a highly attractive object rather than from the specific cognitive process we have envisioned. Hence, we felt it was necessary to have two additional experimental conditions that were treated in exactly the same way as the two mentioned above except for the fact that now the subjects would not be making a decision among the alternatives for themselves. In these two additional conditions the subjects would be asked to say which of the imperfect alternatives they liked best, but there would be no implication that they would get anything. If the mere presence or absence of the very attractive but unavailable alternative produces any difference between the conditions, it seems likely that this effect would be the same irrespective of whether or not the decision was for themselves. If, however, a difference between the conditions is due to our hypothesized pre-decision process, it should affect only those conditions in which the subjects are actually making a decision for themselves.

Procedure

The subjects used in the experiment were 127 boys from the second and third grades of two Palo Alto, California, schools. Each boy came individually to a room to talk to the experimenter, having been previously informed that she was a representative of a toy company. When the boy entered the experimental room he was seated at a small table and told that the experimenter would show him a number of toys because she was interested in knowing whether or not he liked each of them. The boy was then shown a scale that was specially prepared so as to be suitable for boys of this age. This rating scale consisted of six points, each one represented by a square. The most favorable point was represented by a large square labeled "Really crazy about this toy; the nicest one I've ever seen." The most unfavorable point on the scale was represented by an extremely small square labeled "Just hate it; the worst toy I've ever seen." The four intermediate points on the scale were similarly identified by squares of different sizes and appropriate labels. The scale and its use were explained to the boy carefully. All the labels were read to him and it was pointed out that the size of the square increased as the liking for the toy increased. The boys seemed to understand the scale well and none had any difficulty using it.

The experimenter then produced a number of toys, one at a time, and asked the child to point at the position on the scale which described how much he liked or disliked that toy. The child was told that he could examine and try out each toy as much as he wished before making his rating. The first two toys the child was shown and asked to rate were irrelevant to the experiment. They were intended to set the child further at ease and to accus-

tom him to the procedure of doing the ratings. The third toy that
the boy was asked to rate differed, depending on the experimental
condition to which the subject had been assigned. Those boys
who were to be in the condition with an "ideal" but unavailable
alternative were shown a rather large, red, racing-car toy, which
was powered by a gasoline engine. Those subjects who were to be
exposed to a mediocre but unavailable alternative were shown an
ordinary blue sedan toy with no motor at all.

The boy was then shown, and asked to rate, five small racing-
car toys, each with a wind-up motor. Each of these toys was different in color and in detail. Furthermore, each of them had a slight
defect—some scratches, a wheel slightly loose, steering wheel miss-
ing, and the like. As the experimenter produced each of them, one
at a time, she pointed out one very desirable aspect of it and also
pointed out its defect. In order to avoid monotony in the descriptions and in the boys' ratings of these racers, two "filler" toys similar to the practice ones were presented between the third and
fourth of the small racers.

After each car was rated by the child, it was put away out of
sight and the next one produced. After the last car was rated and
put away, the experimenter administered a "Post-Rating Memory
Test." She said to the boy, "You've seen a lot of toys today. I'd
like you to tell me every toy you can remember seeing." The experimenter simply recorded which toys the boy mentioned. No
probing or prodding was done.

The "ideal" toy (or the "mediocre" toy) was then taken out of
the box and placed at the back of the table. The five slightly damaged small racers were placed on the table directly in front of the
boy. The experimental procedure now varied depending upon the
condition to which the subject had been assigned.

Decision Conditions. In these conditions the subject was asked
to choose which of the five slightly damaged racers he wanted as
a free gift for himself. The experimenter said:

O.K., there's one more thing I'd like you to do. Since we get all our toys
free, we decided to give each boy who helped us a toy to thank him for
coming in. We *had* planned to give you this toy [*holding up the "ideal"
or the "mediocre" toy depending upon the experimental condition*], but
then the toy makers changed their minds; they decided *not* to give you
that one. Instead, you can have any of *these* racers that you want. Why
don't you figure out which of the racers you want, and as soon as you
know for sure, tell me and I'll give it to you.

Preference Conditions. In these conditions the subject was asked to state which of the five slightly damaged racers he liked best, but there was no implication that he would receive any toy for himself. The experimenter said:

O.K., there's one more thing I'd like you to do. We *had* planned to ask you about this car [*holding up the "ideal" or the "mediocre" toy depending on the experimental condition*], but then the toy makers changed their minds; they decided *not* to ask you about that one. Instead, we would like to ask you something about *these* racers. The toy makers never know which kind kids will end up liking best. To get some idea, we'd like you to tell us which racer you think is the best. Why don't you figure out which racer you like best, and as soon as you know, tell me and I'll write it down.

In both sets of conditions the experimenter, using a hidden stop watch, measured the time it took from the end of this statement until the boy indicated which toy he wanted (or liked best). The subject was then asked to rate, on the same scale he had used previously, the toy he had chosen.

All subjects in the experiment were given a second memory test in a somewhat different form from the first one described above.

Post-Decision Memory Test. After the choice had been made and the chosen racer had been rated, the boy's chair was turned away from the table, he was asked to shut his eyes, and the experimenter said:

Now you know all the toys that are on the table. Well, the first time I showed them to you, I told you a lot of things about them, and when you played with them, you probably noticed a lot of things about them. I'd like you to tell me everything you can remember about every single toy that's on the table now.

Pre-Decision Memory Test. A memory test before, rather than after, the decision was used for some subjects in the "ideal" alternative conditions only. For these subjects, about four seconds after the choice instructions, the experimenter said: "Oh dear. Close your eyes. I was supposed to ask you one thing before you decide which car you want (or like best)." The experimenter then gave exactly the same instructions as for the post-decision memory test. After the subject had finished, the experimenter said, "O.K., now you can finish deciding which car you want (like best)."

The experimenter recorded which cars were mentioned during

TABLE 6.1

Number of Subjects in Experimental Conditions

	Decision Condition	Preference Condition
"Ideal" Unavailable Alternative		
Pre-Decision Memory Test	11	11
Post-Decision Memory Test	30	23
"Mediocre" Unavailable Alternative		
Pre-Decision Memory Test	Not included in design	
Post-Decision Memory Test	30	22

this second memory test and whether the remarks about each of them were positive or negative. At the conclusion of the session the experimenter told each subject that his gift for helping in the study would be delivered to him the following week. The subjects were asked not to tell their classmates about the experiment.

Altogether, six experimental conditions were run. Subjects were assigned to conditions at random but no attempt was made to have an equal number of subjects in each condition. Rather, more subjects were assigned to those conditions in which we wanted to have more reliable measures. Table 6.1 gives a summary of the design and the number of subjects in each condition.

Results

Before examining the evidence relevant to the main hypothesis of the study, it would be well to check on whether or not we did, indeed, create the experimental conditions that were intended. Two major points are involved here. First, is the "ideal" unavailable alternative really much better than the alternatives that are available and is the "mediocre" unavailable alternative worse than the available ones? Second, can we be reasonably sure that the mere presence of the "ideal" or the "mediocre" car does not in itself, because of the effect of comparison, alter the attractiveness of the five slightly damaged racers? Unless we have evidence on this, we cannot be sure that we have really presented the same decision situation in the two sets of experimental conditions.

On the first point there is really very little question. The "ideal" car was actually an extremely desirable toy and the "mediocre" car was quite undistinguished. The data, of course, bear this out. It will be recalled that the very first thing done in the experiment was to have the subject rate each of the toys on a six-point scale. The average rating given to the "ideal" car (75 subjects) was 1.1, very close to the maximum liking on the scale. The average rating given to the "mediocre" car (52 subjects) was 3.1, close to the point on the scale that was labeled "Like a little more than most toys." The average ratings given by all subjects to the five slightly damaged racers was 2.1, midway between the other two. All of these means differ from one another at very high levels of statistical significance. It is clear that the "ideal" car was seen as more attractive, and the "mediocre" car as less attractive than the alternatives among which they were later to choose.

There is, however, some question concerning the second point of whether or not the attractiveness of the available alternatives was affected by the presence of the "ideal" or the "mediocre" car. There are several sets of data that one can examine in relation to this question. Let us look first at the initial ratings of the five slightly damaged racers. It will be recalled that on the initial ratings, the "ideal" or the "mediocre" car always came before the five racers. Consequently, if having seen and rated the "ideal" or the "mediocre" car affected the attractiveness of the five racers, it might be evident in the initial ratings. The average rating given to the racers by those who saw the "ideal" car (75 subjects) was 2.2; the corresponding average rating given by those who saw the "mediocre" car (52 subjects) was 1.9. The difference between these two means does not come close to an acceptable level of statistical significance, but there is the suspicion, nevertheless, that an effect may have occurred which, for our present purposes, is undesirable. The five slightly damaged racers may, indeed, seem less attractive to those who have seen the "ideal" car.

One can pursue the question by looking at other relevant data. It will be recalled that, after the choice had been made, the subjects were asked to rate, once more, the racer which they had chosen. This occurred, of course, after the "ideal" or the "mediocre" car had been shown to them again, and consequently the effect on the attractiveness of the chosen racer might be even stronger. The average post-decision ratings of the chosen racer are shown in

TABLE 6.2

Average Post-Decision Ratings of Chosen Racer

	Made Decision	Indicated Preference
"Ideal" Unavailable Alternative	1.6	1.6
	(N = 41)	(N = 34)
"Mediocre" Unavailable Alternative	1.4	1.3
	(N = 30)	(N = 22)

Table 6.2. These averages are presented separately for those who were choosing a gift for themselves and for those who were simply indicating a preference.

Again we see the same tendency in the data. Although the differences again do not approach statistical significance, there is once more the suspicion that having seen the "ideal" car makes the slightly damaged racer less attractive.

There is one more set of data relevant to this question. It will be recalled that all subjects were given a second memory test either after the choice had been made or at the beginning of the decision process. On this second memory test they were asked to recall all the characteristics they could remember about each of the cars. The experimenter recorded what they remembered and whether it was a positive or a negative attribute. If the presence of the "ideal" car did make the slightly damaged racers seem less attractive, it might be expected that this would reveal itself in more emphasis on the negative characteristics of the racers. Table 6.3 presents these data for the six experimental conditions. The table gives the average number of characteristics mentioned altogether, and the difference between the number of negative and the number of positive characteristics recalled. In all conditions, more negative than positive characteristics were recalled.

An examination of the figures in Table 6.3 reveals that for the conditions in which the subjects were choosing a racer as a gift for themselves, there is a clear difference in the recall of positive and negative characteristics. In the "ideal" unavailable alternative conditions they recall, on the average, 1.9 and 1.8 more negative than positive characteristics of the five racers. The corresponding figure for the "mediocre" unavailable alternative condition is only

TABLE 6.3

Recall of Positive and Negative Characteristics of the
Five Slightly Damaged Racers

	Decision		Preference	
	Number Recalled	Negative Minus Positive	Number Recalled	Negative Minus Positive
"Ideal" Unavailable Alternative:				
Post-Decision Memory	3.5	1.9	3.2	0.8
Pre-Decision Memory	3.3	1.8	3.1	0.4
"Mediocre" Unavailable Alternative:				
Post-Decision Memory	3.4	1.1	3.8	0.5

1.1. The difference between the "ideal" and the "mediocre" conditions is significant at the 2 per cent level. There are no clear or consistent differences among the "Preference" conditions. Altogether, the subjects in the Preference conditions recall positive and negative characteristics in more nearly equal numbers than do subjects in the "Decision" conditions. Why this should be is not clear. It is possible that, in general, negative characteristics seem more important when a decision is to be made for a gift for oneself. It is also possible that since the instructions in the Preference conditions dwelt on the desire of the manufacturers to know how well children liked these toys, the subjects may have tended to see the slight damages as not a necessary aspect of the racer. When the subject chose the toy he himself wanted to keep, the damages were, of course, inescapable.

Whatever the reason for the difference between the Decision and the Preference conditions, we must accept the conclusion that a difference probably exists in the attractiveness of the available alternatives, depending upon whether the unavailable alternative was "ideal" or "mediocre." In other words, we cannot maintain, unfortunately, that the same decision situation was present psychologically in all conditions. In the "mediocre" unavailable alternative conditions they were making a choice among slightly more attractive alternatives than in the "ideal" unavailable alternative conditions. We will have to bear this in mind as a possible source of alternative interpretations of the results of the experiment.

Let us then turn to an examination of the evidence relevant to the hypothesis that, in order for a decision to be made, the person must first turn his attention away from more attractive, but unavailable, alternatives. A simple, although gross, reflection of such a pre-decision process should be observable in the length of time required to make the decision. If such a process does occur, it should result in longer decision times. Thus, one would expect that when a decision is made in the presence of an "ideal" unavailable alternative, the decision time would be longer, on the average, than when the decision is made in the presence of a "mediocre" unavailable alternative. Furthermore, one would expect that this effect on decision time would be observed only when a decision was to be made, and not when a mere preference was to be stated. In the Preference conditions, where the subject is merely asked to state which he likes best, there is no reason to assume that he must put the "ideal" alternative out of his mind in order to state such a preference.

Table 6.4 presents the data on average decision time for those four experimental conditions in which a meaningful measure of decision time could be obtained. No such measure could be obtained in the two conditions in which the decision process was interrupted in order to administer a pre-decision memory test.

On the whole, the data in Table 6.4 support the hypothesis. The decision time is significantly longer $(t = 2.27, 58$ degrees of freedom) when the subjects choose a toy for themselves in the presence of an "ideal" unavailable alternative than when such a decision is made in the presence of a "mediocre" unavailable alternative. When only a statement of preference is required, rather than a decision, the difference is negligible and not at all significant statistically, although it is in the same direction. An analysis

TABLE 6.4

Average Time (in Seconds) to Make a Decision Among the Five Slightly Damaged Racers

	Decision	Preference
"Ideal" Unavailable Alternative	29.7	13.2
"Mediocre" Unavailable Alternative	18.6	10.2

of variance, however, reveals that the interaction is not significant $(F = 2.85, p = .20)$. In short, while one difference is and the other is not significant, the difference between the differences does not reach an acceptable level. The data, hence, while supporting our hypothesis, are not compelling.

One must also, of course, in interpreting these data, take into account the possibility that at least some of the difference in decision time may be due to differences in the attractiveness of the alternatives rather than to the occurrence or non-occurrence of the hypothesized pre-decision process. After all, there is evidence in the literature (e.g., Barker, 1942) that decisions between unpleasant alternatives take longer than decisions between pleasant alternatives. It is unlikely, however, that this factor could account for the large difference in decision time that we obtained. The difference in attractiveness of the available alternatives depending on whether the "ideal" or the "mediocre" car was present was very small. Also, in all cases the slightly damaged racers were very attractive to the children. However, considering the marginal levels of significance in the data, and considering that at least part of the effect may be due to other factors, we must regard the decision-time data as not conclusive by themselves.

We can, however, look for corroborating evidence in the data obtained in the two memory tests. It will be recalled that the major purpose of these memory tests was to get an indication of the extent to which the "ideal" or the "mediocre" car was salient in the cognition of the subject at various periods with respect to the decision. If our hypothesized pre-decision process does occur and if it is responsible for the increased decision time, we would expect to see evidence that when the "ideal" unavailable alternative is present, and when the decision is to be made for oneself, the "ideal" car should be very salient early in the decision process. By the time the decision is made, however, the subjects should have stopped thinking about it. Such changes in the extent to which they think about the unavailable alternative should not occur if the "mediocre" car is present, or if a preference, rather than a decision, is being stated. Table 6.5 presents the data on the percentage of subjects who mention the unavailable alternative on the various memory tests. It seems plausible to take this as an indication of how salient the unavailable alternative is, at that time, in the cognition of the subject.

TABLE 6.5
Per Cent of Subjects Recalling the Unavailable Alternative

	Memory Test I	Memory Test II Pre-Decision	Memory Test II Post-Decision
"Ideal" Alternative, Decision			
Pre-Decision Memory (N = 11)	64	91	
Post-Decision Memory (N = 30)	83		50
"Ideal" Alternative, Preference			
Pre-Decision Memory (N = 11)	82	73	
Post-Decision Memory (N = 23)	74		83
"Mediocre" Alternative, Decision (N = 30)	37		60
"Mediocre" Alternative, Preference (N = 22)	41		64

If we look at the last two rows in Table 6.5, we may note that the memory for the "mediocre" car presents a rather simple picture. It makes no difference whether a decision is being made or a preference is being stated in the presence of this car. On the first memory test after the initial rating of the toys it turns out that this car is not very memorable—about 40 per cent of the children mention it. This is not surprising, since it is such an undistinguished toy. By the end of the experiment, after the decision or statement of preference, they have seen the car again and more of them—about 60 per cent—remember it.

The data for those subjects who stated a preference in the presence of the "ideal" car present a picture that is not too different. The "ideal" car is, of course, much more immediately memorable. In one condition 82 per cent, and in another condition 74 per cent, mention it on the first memory test. There are no significant changes from these initial figures as the decision process proceeds. At the beginning of the pre-decision period, 73 per cent mention it, and after the decision, 83 per cent mention it. There is no indication of any change.

The memory data for those subjects who made a decision in the presence of the "ideal" unavailable alternative, however, present quite a different pattern. Here again, of course, the "ideal" car turns out to be quite memorable, being remembered by 64 per cent and 83 per cent of the subjects in the two conditions. Early in the pre-decision period, however, there is some tendency for increased memory of the "ideal" car. While seven out of 11 subjects mentioned it on the first memory test, ten out of the 11 mention it on the second memory test in the pre-decision condition. With such a small number of cases the change is, of course, not significant. It is, however, in line with the expectation one would have from the hypothesis.

More conclusive, and more significant statistically, are the data for the post-decision memory. In this condition, 83 per cent mentioned the "ideal" car after the initial rating, but only 50 per cent mention it after the decision has been made. This change is highly significant. Eleven boys who mentioned it on the first test did not mention it on the second one; only one boy mentioned the "ideal" car on the second test who had not mentioned it on the first one. The difference in post-decision memory of the "ideal" car between the decision and the preference conditions is also significant ($\chi^2 = 6.02, p = .02$).

These data support the contention that the subjects in the decision condition had to push the "ideal" unavailable alternative out of their minds in order to make a decision. Given these data on memory, it also seems more plausible to attribute the increased decision time in this condition to the same process.

■

If we allow ourselves to speculate freely about the significance of the experiment by Walster and Festinger that has just been described, we are led to some interesting ideas about the decision-making process. The Walster and Festinger experiment, in and of itself, is frankly preliminary and exploratory. It constitutes an attempt to determine whether a possible psychological process does or does not occur. Although the data are weak in spots, on the whole they provide evidence that the hypothesized process does occur. Let us then accept the proposition that if a person is faced with a decision between imperfect alternatives, he may devote time and effort to a search for better alternatives and may consider possibilities even though he knows they are not available to him.

Such a proposition is interesting but it is certainly not startling. It is perfectly plausible that this process can occur, and the experiment has shown that one can arrange conditions, in a rather obvious manner, so that it is likely to occur. But there is a more interesting aspect to the idea behind the experiment. Usually, when we think about a situation in which a person must decide among two or more alternatives, we analyze the situation, and theorize about it, in terms of the characteristics of the alternatives and the person's behavior with respect to these alternatives. The Walster and Festinger experiment shows, however, that this is too narrow a framework within which to reach an adequate description of pre-decision cognitive processes. The behavior of the person, his considerations and his thought processes, are not confined to the alternatives between which he must decide. Factors outside this narrow realm also affects what he does.

Once we start looking outside the immediate decision situation for factors that affect behavior in the pre-decision period, we can be led in many directions. What, for example, would be the effect on pre-decision cognitive processes of arbitrarily restricting the number of possible alternatives; what kinds of conditions produce impulsive rather than deliberate decisions; in what kinds of circumstances do people refuse to make decisions?

It was natural for us to think of, and to explore, the possible consequences of the anticipation of post-decision dissonance for pre-decision behavior. It is by no means clear to what extent, if at all, in the ordinary course of making a decision, a person anticipates dissonance and reacts to this anticipation. And we have little or no evidence on the basis of which one may specify which variables increase or decrease the likelihood of anticipating dissonance during the pre-decision period. It seems plausible to assert that if a person has experienced considerable post-decision dissonance in the past, he may be more likely to anticipate it and to react to this anticipation. But this kind of assertion is not very helpful.

There are some things, however, that can be said in spite of all this unclarity. If a person anticipates dissonance as a consequence of making a decision, he would be expected to react by attempting to minimize, or to avoid completely, the anticipated dissonance. There are a limited number of ways in which the person may seek to do this. He may, in the pre-decision period, attempt to persuade himself that the decision is of little importance, or he may try to avoid making the decision altogether. If the decision is of little importance, there will generally be less post-decision dissonance. To the extent that the person can avoid the responsibility for making the decision, he also avoids the post-decision dissonance.

It is clearly possible to test these ideas in a laboratory experiment. Regardless of how prevalent the anticipation of dissonance is in the ordinary decision situation, we can certainly create an experimental condition in which we can be sure that dissonance is anticipated. If we set up such an experiment so that the magnitude of the anticipated dissonance is rather independent of the importance of the decision, then the following prediction is clear. In a condition in which the person anticipated dissonance as a consequence of making a decision we should observe some reluctance to make the decision. If the situation is such that it is easy to avoid making the decision, we would expect to observe such avoidance. Braden and Walster report such an experiment below.

Experiment

The Effect of Anticipated Dissonance on Pre-Decision Behavior

Marcia Braden and Elaine Walster

There are times when a person will avoid making a decision even though he has a preference between the alternatives. Sometimes, for example, a person in a restaurant, after staring at the menu for some time, will breathe a clear sigh of relief if her companion offers to order for her. A high school graduate faced with a choice between two colleges may sometimes almost beg his parents to tell him which one to choose. Such reluctance to make a decision is not rare.

There are at least two possible explanations for this reluctance.

It is plausible to suppose that the conflict situation itself is somewhat unpleasant. If this is true, then one can interpret the avoidance of a decision as a means of avoiding, or escaping from, the conflict. The other possible explanation involves the anticipation of post-decision dissonance. Even though dissonance does not exist until after the decision is made, a person may react to the anticipation of such dissonance because through previous experience he has learned to be wary of it. One way to avoid any post-decision dissonance is to avoid making a decision.

Both of these explanations may be correct; that is, both processes may play a part in producing avoidance of decision making. There is, however, no clear evidence that either of these processes does, in fact, occur. This experiment represents an attempt to determine whether or not one can observe decision avoidance as a reaction solely to the anticipation of dissonance. We will not concern ourselves with the possible unpleasantness of conflict except to see to it that this factor does not play a differential role in the experiment.

The design of this experiment is quite simple. There are two experimental conditions. In both of them, subjects are faced with the identical decision. In one condition the situation is described so as to increase the anticipation of dissonance. In the other condition, with instructions held as constant as possible, the anticipation of dissonance is not encouraged. One should observe more frequent refusal to make a decision in the former condition. In order to ensure that the measurements would be sensitive enough, the experimental situation was arranged so that it was easy to refuse to make the decision.

Procedure

Forty-two high school girls were used as subjects in the experiment. The girls volunteered to participate in a "survey conducted by a company that produced popular phonograph records." They were told that they would be paid one dollar for participating in the survey.

Each girl was interviewed individually. When she arrived for the interview she was told that we were interested in finding out some things about teenagers' preferences. She was then shown the names of 13 popular singers and asked to rank them from most liked to least liked. The purpose of this, apart from lending credibility to the ostensible purpose of the "survey," was to obtain some indication of the extent to which the girls liked one particular singer whose name was identified with the two records between which they would later be asked to choose.

The experimenter then engaged in an elaborate explanation of a "new promotion technique" that the company sponsoring the survey was about to use. The purpose of this explanation was simply to set the stage for the manipulation of anticipated dissonance. The experimenter explained that movies and plays were often reviewed and that quotations from the reviews, used in advertising, were successful in attracting new viewers. The record company had decided to use a similar promotional technique—they were going to print quotations from reviews on the labels of two records that were soon to be released. These quotations were to be recommendations from high school girls about the records.

The experimenter then drew the girl's attention to two stacks of records on the table. One of these stacks of records had green labels and the record was titled "The Stranger"; the other stack had white labels bearing the title "Forgetting You." The same singer was listed as the recording artist on both records. The subject was told that these were advance copies of the records. They had not yet been released, so the girl, of course, had not heard either of the songs. Before releasing them, the company was trying to find out which quotations from high school girls' recommendations would be most effective in selling each record. Last week, in order to get some quotations for possible use, these records had been played to girls in a different high school and those girls had written recommendations for the record they especially liked. Two lists of very enthusiastic recommendations, one list for each of the two records, now existed.

The experimenter continued, explaining that the next step was to discover which of these recommendations would be best to use for advertising on the labels of the records when they were released. The plan was to assemble a large number of small groups, four girls to a group, and to read to each group the recommendations for one of these records. Each group would then vote on which recommendation would most make them want to hear and buy the record being described. The best way to obtain honest and helpful votes from such groups was to have someone their own age meet with each group, read the list of recommendations, and get the votes. This procedure, they were told, had turned out to be most successful. The experimenter then asked the girl if she would be willing to help out by reading the list of recommendations about *one* of the records to four different groups of girls during the next two weeks. After the girl agreed to do this (and they all did) actual appointment times were set up.

The experimenter then proceeded to create a situation in which subjects were asked to make a decision under circumstances in which they either did, or did not, anticipate that dissonance would ensue. To create a condition of "anticipated dissonance," the experimenter said:

As you can see from the stacks of records here on the table, we have lots of copies of the two records. We decided we might as well give one to each girl who helps us out by reading one of the lists of recommendations to four groups of other girls. Before you leave today, we'll flip a coin to determine which of the two records you'll be given as a gift.

Since you'll be reading recommendations about only one of these records to other girls, it seemed to us that you could probably do a better and fairer job during the next two weeks if you read the list of enthusiastic recommendations about the record which you do *not* get yourself. That means that if, on the coin toss, you get this record [*pointing to one*], it will be your job to read the things students really like about this record [*pointing to the other one*], and vice versa.

Oh, golly, wait a minute! Just yesterday we decided that if any of the students helping us had any special preference for one or the other of the records, she could *choose* which one she wanted. Naturally, if you choose a record, you will then read the things people liked best about the record you didn't choose. If you don't want to decide which one you like best, we can still flip a coin as we planned before. What would you like to do?

To create an experimental condition of "anticipated consonance," subjects were given the identical instructions in the identical order except that throughout they were told that they would read the recommendations about the record they *received* to the groups of other girls. When they were told that they could choose a record, they were told that if they did so, they would read the list of recommendations about the record they chose. Thus, the only difference between the two conditions was whether they expected to read a list of statements extolling the record they would possess, or one extolling the record they would not possess.

Next, either the girl chose a record, or a coin was flipped, as she desired. She was then asked to rate each of the two records on a nine-point scale on which 1 was labeled "Think I will like it extremely much," and 9 represented "Think I will dislike it very much."

The experiment was then explained to each girl, and she was paid one dollar for participating.

Results

Two experimental conditions were created in the experiment, one of anticipated dissonance and one of anticipated consonance. Actually, of course, these designations of the experimental conditions are correct only if the subject chooses which record she wants. Reading enthusiastic recommendations for an alternative that one has rejected may be expected to create dissonance. Reading such recommendations about a record one does not own because of the toss of a coin certainly does not create any dissonance. Consequently, if the subject reacts in anticipation of dissonance, one would expect a higher incidence of unwillingness to choose in the anticipated-dissonance condition. The experimental situation was designed, of course, to make it easy for the subject to avoid making the choice. First, there was little basis for making a choice. The singer was the same on both records, and they did not hear the records. Only the different titles could provide a basis for choosing. In addition, not choosing was described as a normal and usual procedure so as to make it easy for the girl to say she would rather flip a coin.

Given the ease of avoiding a choice, one may expect that any difference between the two conditions in reluctance to choose would be adequately reflected in the relative frequency of avoiding choice. These data are presented in Table 6.6. It is clear from the table that where consonance is anticipated, in spite of the meager basis for choosing, the great majority (81 per cent) make such a choice rather than leave the matter to chance. This, of course, is what one would expect and seems quite sensible. Even if only a slight preference exists, why not make a choice? When

TABLE 6.6

Number of Subjects Who Make or Avoid a Decision

	Anticipated Dissonance	Anticipated Consonance
Choose a Record	6	17
Flip a Coin	15	4

dissonance is anticipated, however, the data are reversed. In this condition 71 per cent want to flip a coin. The difference between the two conditions is highly significant statistically ($\chi^2 = 11.63$). In short, if dissonance is anticipated as a direct consequence of making a decision, there is a decided tendency to avoid the decision.

The data seem rather clear and it is difficult to think of other possible reasons for the difference between the two conditions. The subjects were assigned at random to the experimental conditions and, on the one pre-measure we obtained, are quite comparable. The average rank of the singer associated with the two records (out of 13 singers) was 4.2 and 4.5 for the anticipated-consonance and anticipated-dissonance conditions, respectively. In other words, the singer was rather well liked, and about equally so in both conditions.

One can also examine whether the difference in experimental procedure made any difference in how well the girls expected to like the records. If it did make a difference, this might be a clue to alternative interpretations. The average rating, on a nine-point scale, was 4.2 in the anticipated-consonance, and 4.1 in the anticipated-dissonance condition. The girls expect to like the records moderately. But again, there is no difference between the conditions.

It is possible, of course, that linking the anticipated dissonance to the choice brought the two alternatives closer together in attractiveness; that is, the girls may have been faced with a decision between "having the better record and doing something unpleasant" and "having the inferior record and doing something pleasant." This, if it made the alternatives nearly equal, could result in difficulty in choosing, which subjects expressed by refusing to choose. If this explanation were correct, however, one would expect a fair number of the girls in the anticipated-dissonance condition to have chosen the inferior record, since, for some, the "unpleasant" action versus "pleasant" action difference would outweigh the difference in attractiveness of the records. This did not occur. It seems reasonable to conclude that the avoidance of decision was, indeed, a consequence of anticipated dissonance.

■

We have presented some evidence in this chapter that the pre-decision period can, and probably should, be viewed as involving more than a mere process of choosing between alternatives. It seems clear from the Walster and Festinger experiment that, strictly speaking, not all of the time consumed in the pre-decision period is spent in the process of deciding. That is, it is not all spent in the process of comparing and evaluating the available alternatives. Some time is spent in considering other more attractive alternatives, even though these may be unavailable. It seems equally clear from the Braden and Walster experiment that willingness or unwillingness to make a decision is affected not solely by the difficulty of the decision or by aspects of the conflict itself. The anticipation of post-decision dissonance produces a heightened reluctance to choose.

Both of the experiments reported in this chapter are preliminary in nature. They are, in a sense, demonstrations that these two effects do occur. The experiments do not contribute much to an understanding of the variables that would determine the magnitude of these effects, nor do they contribute much to an understanding of how factors outside the immediate decision situation interact with the conflict in which the person finds himself. Perhaps, however, these demonstrations will help open the way for such new understanding.

Chapter Seven

Conclusions and Problems

■

We have presented the results of ten experiments, all of which are focused on the problem of understanding the decision process. They are all concerned with elucidating either what goes on during the period in which a person is making a decision or how a person behaves after the decision has been made. It is worthwhile at this time to review what new understanding we have acquired as a result of these ten experiments. It will also be useful to see what problems exist with respect to the data and the interpretations of the data. We will do this by giving a sequential picture, as we see it now, of the decision process—from conflict, through decision, to dissonance. In part, this sequential picture will summarize the data we have obtained. In part, it will be speculation.

When a person is faced with a decision between two alternatives, his behavior is largely oriented toward making an objective and impartial evaluation of the merits of the alternatives. This behavior probably takes the form of collecting information about the alternatives, evaluating this information in relation to himself, and establishing a preference order between the alternatives. Establishing a preference order does not immediately result in a decision. The person probably continues to seek new information and to re-evaluate old information until he acquires sufficient confidence that his preference order will not be upset and reversed by subsequent information. This continued information seeking and information evaluation remains, however, objective and impartial.

When the required level of confidence is reached, the person makes a decision. Undoubtedly, the closer together in attractiveness the alternatives are, the more important the decision, and the more variable the information about the alternatives, the higher is the confidence that the person will want before he makes his decision. It is probably this process of seeking and evaluating information that consumes time when a person must make a decision.

What evidence do we have to support the above statement? The data concerning the objectivity and impartiality of the pre-decision process are rather consistent. In Chapter 4, Jecker reports data showing that before the decision is made the person spends equal amounts of time reading favorable and unfavorable information about the alternative he eventually chooses. In Chapter 2, Davidson and Kiesler and also Jecker present data which show that throughout the pre-decision period there is no noticeable divergence in the attractiveness of the two alternatives involved in the decision. In short, there is no evidence of any biasing influences before the decision is made. Of particular importance in supporting this conclusion are the two experiments by Jecker in which subjects in some conditions made decisions but were uncertain of the effect their decisions would have on the outcome. In these conditions we can be quite certain that measurements were taken after the pre-decision period was completed, and yet, in these conditions, the evidence is uniform in indicating the impartiality of information seeking and the absence of any systematic, biasing re-evaluation of alternatives.

Evidence that the pre-decision activity is concerned, to a large extent, with gathering and evaluating information is more tangential. No experiments specifically designed to test this notion were reported, but in Chapters 2 and 3 some data are reported which can reasonably be interpreted in this manner. It will be recalled that in Chapter 3 Davidson reports an experiment which shows that the more a person has thought over the relevant details before dissonance is aroused, the more rapidly does dissonance reduction proceed after the dissonance has been introduced. It will further be recalled that this experiment was done in order to help understand the incidental findings reported in Chapter 2 that the more time the person spent thinking about the alternatives in the pre-decision period, the greater was the amount of dissonance reduction in the post-decision period. Considering all the data, the most plausible interpretation of these results is that the more carefully the person thinks through and evaluates information beforehand,

the more rapidly can dissonance reduction proceed once dissonance is aroused. If this interpretation is true, then there is some
inferential evidence that in the pre-decision period the person does
spend his time considering and evaluating information about the
alternatives.

Seeking and evaluating information about the alternatives is,
however, not the only thing that occurs in the pre-decision period.
We will not speculate much about all the possibilities here. The
experiments we have reported have only touched the surface of
this problem, and it is clear that much remains to be understood.
It certainly seems plausible to maintain that the decision maker
is not a passive person, meekly accepting the decision situation as
the environment poses it for him. Certainly, if the alternatives are
not to his liking, he will search for other, better alternatives. If
there are inevitable unpleasant consequences of making a decision,
he will try to avoid making it. Both of these effects have been illus-
trated by the experiments reported in Chapter 6.

There is, however, one aspect of the pre-decision period about
which we would like to speculate briefly. The pre-decision process,
as we described it above, sounds like a very sane and rational
process. And our data tend to support the idea that this is the way
many decisions are made, at least those decisions with which a person is faced in an experimental situation. But casual observation,
our own experience, and our intuition lead us to believe that
occasionally, perhaps frequently, decisions are made on a rather
impulsive basis. There are times when a person makes a decision,
even an important one, very quickly, without considering much
information about the alternatives. There are even instances when,
after careful and thorough consideration of information about the
alternatives, the person seems to make his decision on the basis
of some minor, almost trivial, aspect. We have little understanding at present of when, and under what conditions, such impulsive
decisions are made. Perhaps such behavior is a means of avoiding
a situation that promises to be a difficult one. If this were the case,
one would expect such impulsive decisions more frequently if the
decision is important and the person thinks the alternatives would
prove to be very close together in attractiveness. Perhaps such impulsive decisions are made when the information-gathering process
seems almost endless. If this were the case, one would expect a

greater frequency of impulsive decisions in instances where the person is faced with a large number of alternatives. Until we know more about these matters, our understanding of the pre-decision situation will remain sketchy.

Once the decision is made and the person is committed to a given course of action, the psychological situation changes decisively. There is less emphasis on objectivity and there is more partiality and bias in the way in which the person views and evaluates the alternatives. Let us be clear about the nature of the change. It is not that suddenly all objectivity disappears. In Chapter 4 we saw clearly that although there is a tendency in the Jecker experiment to look more at consonant than at dissonant material in the post-decision period, this tendency is small and is easily overcome by other factors. In the same chapter, Canon showed that although there is clearly a tendency in the post-decision period to prefer consonant to dissonant material and to attempt to reduce dissonance, the potential usefulness of dissonant material can readily overcome this other tendency. Certainly, objectivity remains, but something more is added—namely, dissonance and the pressure to reduce the dissonance.

Let us also be clear about the circumstances under which dissonance reduction begins. The two experiments by Jecker, one reported in Chapter 2 and the other in Chapter 4, together with the experiment reported by Allen in Chapter 3, force us to reconsider the nature, and the consequences, of making a decision. Festinger (1957) clearly states that making a decision arouses dissonance and pressures to reduce the dissonance. But these experiments clearly indicate that even after a decision is made, there is no evidence of dissonance reduction if there is no definite commitment resulting from the decision. The Jecker experiment reported in Chapter 4 shows that if the subject does not know whether his decision will have any bearing at all on what happens, there is no selective exposure to information and no evidence at all of any dissonance-reduction process. The Jecker experiment in Chapter 2 shows likewise that there is an absence of any dissonance reduction after a choice between two alternatives if the person does not know whether he will get only the chosen alternative or both of them. The Allen experiment in Chapter 3 replicates this finding and shows that significant dissonance reduction is obtained after the choice only if the person has definitely, by his decision, given up the unchosen alternative. On the whole, the evidence is clear that simply making a decision does not guarantee the onset of dissonance-reduction processes.

In the light of these findings one is led to accept the emphasis on commitment proposed by Brehm and Cohen (1962). These authors, reviewing the theory of dissonance and the research relevant to it, come to the conclusion that " . . . under conditions where commitment is present, dissonance does clearly occur and produce its effects on cognition . . . " (Page 300.) Although Brehm and Cohen are somewhat vague with respect to the conceptual meaning of commitment, we can perhaps add some specificity to it here. It seems that a decision carries commitment with it if the decision unequivocally affects subsequent behavior. This is not intended to mean that the decision is irrevocable, but rather that the decision has clear implication for the subsequent unrolling of events as long as the person stays with that decision.

This perhaps casts some light on the psychological difference between a "statement of preference" and a "decision." A person might look at two paintings in an exhibition and say that he likes one of them better than the other. He has expressed a preference, but unless the circumstances are unusual, there are no consequences flowing from this statement of preference. If, however, he is shown these two paintings and the artist tells him that whichever he likes better is his to keep as a gift, then a decision is made. One of the paintings, the one he prefers, is now his. The world, in a sense, has been changed by the decision—consequences follow and commitment exists. Dissonance reduction can now be expected to occur.

In the absence of data it is probably not fruitful to speculate too much about this. If these ideas are valid, it should not prove difficult to provide experimental evidence that can clarify them and help support further theoretical speculation. Let us, then, return to our consideration of the decision process itself. Once the decision is made which carries commitment with it, how does the psychological situation change and how do dissonance-reduction processes start?

From the data that we have presented, it seems plausible to maintain that in the immediate post-decision period, dissonance becomes salient. That is, as soon as the decision is made, the person's attention becomes focused on the cognitions that are now dissonant with the chosen course of action. Dissonance reduction undoubtedly proceeds by thinking about, considering and reconsidering, and re-evaluating these dissonant cognitions until adequate reinterpretations are invented or discovered. There is a period, however, between the making of the decision and the time that dissonance reduction becomes effective, during which the person may experience regret. There are certainly many post-decision situations in which dissonance reduction is easy and the period of regret is so brief as to pass unmarked. If, however, dissonance reduction is difficult to accomplish, there may be considerable time during which the person continues to focus on the dissonance without being able to reduce it materially.

One can well imagine that the very act of focusing on, and continuing to consider the dissonant cognitions would make these cognitions seem more and more important. Thus, until dissonance reduction becomes effective, there can be a period in which the chosen alternative and the rejected alternative draw closer and closer together in attractiveness. In Chapter 5, we have presented evidence that such a state of regret does indeed intervene between the decision and the beginning of successful dissonance reduction. Festinger and Walster present data that show the existence of a strong tendency toward decision reversal in the immediate post-decision period, which can be interpreted as a manifestation of the salience of unreduced dissonance. Walster presents data which go farther in that she attempts to get measurements at different time intervals following the decision, so that the course of regret and dissonance reduction may be plotted through time. She does, indeed, find clear evidence of a regret period during which the alternatives draw closer together in attractiveness. This is followed by the expected increased divergence in attractiveness of the alternatives; that is, dissonance reduction does proceed after the regret period.

The data from the Walster experiment, however, present problems. Walster found clear and significant evidence of dissonance reduction by 15 minutes after the decision, but this evidence did not persist. Ninety minutes after the decision, the separation in attractiveness of the alternatives had reverted to its pre-decision level. Why this occurred, and what its implications are, is not clear. It is possible that this is a consequence of the fact that dissonance reduction in the situation was very difficult and that the subjects were kept isolated and deprived of any possible external aids for reducing dissonance. After all, in order to produce a measurable period of regret, Walster deliberately tried to create a situation in which dissonance reduction would be quite difficult. It may very well be that in such a situation, without social support and without additional sources of information, dissonance reduction does not prove to be very stable. Outside support may be necessary to help the person continue to believe what he wants to believe.

The Walster finding makes us realize acutely that there is an entire set of important problems that have been ignored in experimental work. We know little about the conditions under which dissonance reduction is easy or difficult and little about the conditions under which dissonance reduction will be stable and lasting. In a natural, uncontrolled situation, once a person has made a decision, events frequently conspire to assist the dissonance-reduction process. For example, let us imagine a person who on graduating from school is offered two jobs, one of which he chooses. This choice makes a great difference in his subsequent behavior. He actually works on the job he chose and not on the one he rejected. He thus has an opportunity to make the chosen job more interesting by the way he works at it. He is not dependent on cognitive manipulations alone to reduce dissonance. In addition, he meets people at work who will undoubtedly help him to believe that the job he chose is a very good one. After all, these people with whom he now associates are working in the same place. It may be that without such changes in the "real world" to support the reduction of dissonance, instability results.

There is an old joke, which is not very funny, about the monograph that concludes by saying that it has created more problems than it has solved. We have, however, in this book added some new knowledge, and the new problems that we have created are, we hope, at least amenable to experimental work.

Adams, J. S. (1961) Reduction of cognitive dissonance by seeking consonant information. *J. abnorm. soc. Psychol.*, **62**, 74–78.

Barker, R. G. (1942) An experimental study of the resolution of conflict by children. In Q. McNemar and M. A. Merrill (Eds.), *Studies in personality*. New York: McGraw-Hill.

Berlyne, D. E. (1960) *Conflict, arousal and curiosity*. New York: McGraw-Hill.

Brehm, J. W. (1956) Post-decision changes in the desirability of alternatives. *J. abnorm. soc. Psychol.*, **52**, 384–89.

Brehm, J. W., and Cohen, A. R. (1959) Re-evaluation of choice alternatives as a function of their number and qualitative similarity. *J. abnorm. soc. Psychol.*, **58**, 373–78.

Brehm, J. W., and Cohen, A. R. (1962) *Explorations in cognitive dissonance*. New York: Wiley.

Brehm, J. W., Cohen, A. R., and Sears, D. (1960) Persistence of post-choice dissonance reduction effects. Unpublished study.

Brock, T. C. (1963) Effects of prior dishonesty on post-decisional dissonance. *J. abnorm. soc. Psychol.*, **66**, 325–31.

Davis, K., and Jones, E. E. (1960) Changes in interpersonal perception as a means of reducing cognitive dissonance. *J. abnorm. soc. Psychol.*, **61**, 402–10.

Ehrlich, D., Guttman, I., Schonbach, P., and Mills, J. (1957) Post-decision exposure to relevant information. *J. abnorm. soc. Psychol.*, **54**, 98–102.

Engel, J. F. (1963) Are automobile purchasers dissonant consumers? *J. Marketing*, **27**, 55–58.

Feather, N. T. (1963a) Cigarette smoking and lung cancer: A study of cognitive dissonance. *Aust. J. Psychol.*, **14**, 55–64.

Feather, N. T. (1963b) Cognitive dissonance, sensitivity, and evaluation. *J. abnorm. soc. Psychol.*, **66**, 157–63.

Festinger, L. (1957) *A theory of cognitive dissonance.* Stanford, Calif.: Stanford University Press.

Irwin, F. W., and Smith, W. A. S. (1956) Further tests of theories of decision in an "expanded judgment" situation. *J. exp. Psychol.,* **52**, 345–48.

Irwin, F. W., Smith, W. A. S., and Mayfield, Jane F. (1956) Tests of two theories of decision in an "expanded judgment" situation. *J. exp. Psychol.,* **51**, 261–68.

Janis, I. L. (1959) Motivational factors in the resolution of decisional conflicts. In M. R. Jones (Ed.), *Nebraska symposium on motivation.* Vol. 8. Lincoln: University of Nebraska Press.

Lewin, K. (1935) *A dynamic theory of personality.* New York: McGraw-Hill.

Lewin, K. (1938) *The conceptual representation and the measurement of psychological forces.* Durham, N.C.: Duke University Press.

Lewin, K. (1951) *Field theory in social science.* D. Cartwright (Ed.), New York: Harper.

Miller, N. E. (1944) Experimental studies of conflict. In J. McV. Hunt (Ed.), *Personality and the behavior disorders.* New York: Ronald.

Mills, J., Aronson, E., and Robinson, H. (1959) Selectivity in exposure to information. *J. abnorm. soc. Psychol.,* **59**, 250–53.

Restle, F. (1961) *Psychology of judgment and choice.* New York: Wiley.

Rosen, S. (1961) Post-decision affinity for incompatible information. *J. abnorm. soc. Psychol.,* **63**, 188–90.

Index

Adams, J. S., 74

Allen, V., v, 34, 42, 155; experiment conducted by, 34–42

alternatives: attractiveness affected by contrast, 136–38; complexity of, 2; consideration of, 11, 17, 31, 44, 97, 108, 132, 152f; divergence as reaction to dissonance, 19; mutual exclusiveness of, 22, 25; narrowing of divergence between, 127; number of, 144; positive or negative, 3, 34, 113f, 117, 126; post-decision divergence in attractiveness, 8, 26, 61, 113; pre-decision divergence in attractiveness, 4, 6, 129, 153; re-evaluation of, 10, 14, 21, 29–32, 97, 107, 153; search for new, 130, 143, 154; unavailable, 130–144, 151; unpleasant, 141

ambiguity of interpretation, 20

Aronson, E., 63, 84, 94

avoidance: of decisions, 145–49, 150, 154; of information, 65, 82–85, 93, 96

Barker, R. G., 25, 141

Berlyne, D. E., 25

Braden, M., v, 151; experiment conducted by, 145–51

Brehm, J. W., 6, 10, 25, 34, 65, 98, 100, 156

Brock, T. C., 6

Canon, L. K., vi, 83, 95f, 155; experiment conducted by, 83–95

choice: between unpleasant alternatives, 141; perception of, 50–57

choice inversion, 25, 35, 38, 40; related to post-decision regret, 101, 105, 108f, 121, 123, 151

cognition: attention to, 98, 108–9, 126, 128; content of, 132; salience of, 98–112, 141, 156f

cognitive processes: details of, 43, 61, 144; interruption of, 61f; measurement of, 61; pre-decision versus post-decision, 4f, 8, 16, 19, 30; sequence of, 112; transition between, 97

Cohen, A. R., 6, 10, 25, 34, 65, 98, 100, 156

confederates, 67, 72

confidence in ability, 82–85, 89, 92–96

conflict: behavior during, 3, 77, 129; magnitude of, 43; resolution, 6, 10, 19f, 27; theory of, 21, 29; unpleasantness of, 6, 146

critical attitude, 82, 85

Davidson, J. R., vi, 9, 19f, 30f, 43ff, 59, 153; experiments conducted by, 10–18, 45–59

Davis, K., 46, 59

decision: act of, 97; avoidance of, 145–51, 154; commitment to, 6, 33f, 38, 40, 42, 155f; confidence in, 3f, 88, 129, 152f; consequences of, 66, 154; context for, 144, 151; difficulty of, 3, 88, 150f; group, 4; implicit, 9, 11, 14, 20; importance of, 112–14, 126, 145, 152; impulsive, 144, 154; overt, 104; point of, 9, 20, 22; responsibility for, 43, 45; reversal, 100–111, 127, 157; tentative, 17; uncertainty of outcome of, 32–35, 38, 40, 67, 71f, 78, 153, 155

decision making, 17, 129f, 143; under pressure, 43, 46, 101, 111

decision process, sequence of, 142, 151f